P9-DXS-367

A history of English spelling

*The series of volumes, of which this is the third,
is inscribed to the memory of Dr Mont Follick*

General editor W. Haas

Mont Follick
series
Volume three

D.G.Scragg   A history of English spelling

Manchester University Press

Barnes & Noble Books · New York
(a division of Harper & Row Publishers, Inc.)

DISCARD

PE 1141
S 3

© 1974   D. G. Scragg
All rights reserved

Published by
Manchester University Press
Oxford Road
Manchester M13 9PL

ISBN 0 7190 0553 1

Published in the U.S.A. 1974 by
Harper & Row Publishers, Inc.
Barnes & Noble Import Division

ISBN 06 496138 9

Printed in Great Britain at
The University Press, Aberdeen

Contents

Illustrations

Acknowledgements

I am grateful to many friends and colleagues for help over minor points in the preparation of this history, including a number of those who heard the Mont Follick Trust lecture in the University of Manchester out of which the book has grown. My thanks are due particularly to Mr J. R. D. Milroy of Queen's University, Belfast, and to Miss Joy Watkin of my own department for their comments on a draft version of the book, and to Professor Haas, who has offered advice, suggestions and encouragement at all stages of its development. I am indebted also to the Master and Fellows of Corpus Christi College, Cambridge, to the Master and Fellows of Gonville and Caius College, Cambridge, and to the Dean and Chapter of Salisbury Cathedral for permission to consult manuscripts in their care, and to the editors of the *Daily Express* and *The Guardian* for permission to quote from their style-sheets. Mr H. C. T. Lindsay helped with the maps, while the plates and figures are reproduced by courtesy of the following: the Syndics of Cambridge University Library (plate 1), the Bodleian Library (figure 1 and plate 4), the Trustees of the British Museum (plates 2, 3 and 5, and figures 3 and 4), the John Rylands University Library of Manchester (figures 2, 5, 6 and 7).

D.G.S.

Abbreviations and signs

OE	Old English, the language recorded from the eighth century to the twelfth
ME	Middle English, the language recorded from the twelfth century to the end of the fifteenth
Mod. E	Modern English, the language recorded from the sixteenth century to the present day
OFr.	Old French, the language up to the end of the fifteenth century
(Mod.) Fr.	(Modern) French
RP	Received Pronunciation, the pronunciation favoured by educated speakers in south-eastern England
⟨ ⟩	denotes a grapheme, a group of symbols which collectively contrast with other symbols in a writing system, e.g. a, ɑ, A as against b, ƀ, B, etc.
/ /	denotes a phoneme, a group of sounds which collectively contrast with other sounds in a given language, e.g. the initial sounds of *keep, carp, coop* as against those of *heap, harp, hoop*, etc.
[]	denotes an allophone, the phonetic realisation of one of the sounds representing the same phoneme, e.g. the initial sound of *coop* [kᵘ] and that of *keep* [kˡ], representing the same phoneme /k/
*	denotes a hypothetical or unrecorded form.

Phonetic symbols

For a full explanation of the terminology of phonetics used in this book see A. C. Gimson, *An Introduction to the Pronunciation of English*, London 1962. In phonetic and phonemic transcription consonant symbols b d f h k l m n p r s t v w z have the value usually associated with them in English. Other symbols have the value indicated below, the pronunciation of the key-words being that of educated speakers of southern British English unless otherwise stated.

g *g*irl
ŋ si*ng*
θ *th*in
ð *th*en
ʃ *sh*in
ʒ mea*s*ure
tʃ *ch*in
dʒ *g*in
j *y*acht
ʍ *wh*ine, when contrasted with *w*ine
ʀ Fr. *r*ouge (voiced uvular roll)
ɣ OE bu*g*an (voiced velar fricative)
ç German i*ch*, Scots li*ch*t (voiceless palatal fricative)
x German a*ch*, Scots lo*ch* (voiceless velar fricative)
₀ subscript denotes breath (e.g. l̥ = voiceless l)
~ superscript denotes nasality (e.g. ã, Fr. bl*a*nc)

Vowels
i s*ee*, Fr. p*i*s
y Fr. l*u*ne (close rounded front vowel)
ɪ s*i*t
e s*e*t, Fr. l*é*gion
ε Fr. l*ai*t (half open front vowel)

æ   h*a*t
ɑ   h*a*rd, Fr. p*a*s
ɒ   h*o*t
ɔ   s*o*rt
ʌ   b*u*t
o   Fr. m*o*t (half close back vowel)
ø   the first vowel in Fr. *légion* with lip-rounding (half close rounded front vowel)
œ   the vowel in Fr. *lait* with lip-rounding (half open rounded front vowel)
ʊ   p*u*ll
u   p*oo*l, Fr. t*ou*t
ə   *a*bout (half open central vowel)
ɜ   bird (central vowel between half-close and half-open position)
:   indicates that the vowel is long

Diphthongs
   eɪ   name
   aɪ   time
   oʊ   home
   ɔɪ   boy
   ɑʊ   house

Chapter 1   The foundation

In the fifth century A.D. the Celtic and Romano-British inhabitants of Britain were subjugated by waves of Germanic settlers from the continent, the majority of whom belonged to two tribes, the Angles and the Saxons. The Germanic dialect spoken by the invaders, who are referred to generically as the Anglo-Saxons, gradually developed characteristics which distinguished it from other varieties of the common Germanic tongue, and it is convenient to term this language English from the time of the migrations to Britain. The history of English orthography begins somewhat later, when Roman and Irish missionaries converted the Anglo-Saxons to Christianity and introduced them to the roman alphabet and its use on parchment at the end of the sixth century. But though no written samples of English have survived from the two centuries between the migration of the Anglo-Saxons to Britain and their conversion to Christianity, the technique of writing was not unknown to them. Long before the invasion of Britain, all of the Germanic tribes wrote in the runic alphabet, and though runic remains in England all date from a comparatively late period (seventh century onwards), there is evidence to suggest that the Anglo-Saxons brought the alphabet with them in the fifth century. Runes had been adapted some centuries before the birth of Christ from a North Italian variety of the common European alphabet, and their relationship with the characters of the roman alphabet may be seen in the form of some of the letters, e.g. ⟨f⟩ and ⟨r⟩ in the contemporary name for the alphabet ᚠᚢᚦᚩᚱᚳ F–U–TH–O–R–C. The particular feature of the futhorc, that which distinguishes it from other European versions of the alphabet, is that it consists of letters formed of straight lines, particularly useful for carving on wood, stone or bone. The early use of runes is not strictly part of this history of orthography in that there is no development in England from rune-carving to writing in the roman alphabet in Christian times. But in later centuries, once the runes had lost their pagan overtones, there was a slight resurgence of interest in them. English runic remains have been found dating from as late as the tenth century, and, in the eleventh, runes were occasionally incorporated into manuscript writings for their antiquarian interest or to draw attention to acrostics, and some were used rather more widely as abbreviations (e.g. the M-rune appears for its name, the common word *man*). More significantly for the history of English orthography, two runes were adapted to supplement the roman alphabet as used in England, supplying characters to represent sounds which did not form part of the phonemic system of Latin. The more important of these is the third letter of the futhorc, ⟨þ⟩, known as thorn, a form found in manuscripts from the end of the eighth century as one of the representatives of the voiced and voiceless dental fricatives /ð/ and /θ/. Thorn remained in use in English writings for nearly a thousand years. It was gradually replaced in Middle English[1] by ⟨th⟩, the grapheme used in Latin to transcribe Greek theta,[2] but in the fifteenth century, when the printing press was introduced from the continent, it was still sufficiently widely used to constitute a problem for compositors with no such character in their continental type. Caxton, the first English printer, used ⟨th⟩ usually, but occasionally compromised by using thorn's nearest typographical equivalent, ⟨y⟩.[3] Thus thorn survived in private papers and in some printed books until the seventeenth century, particularly in contractions of the definite article and the demonstrative adjective, *y^e*, *y^t* 'the, that', and may be seen still in pseudo-archaic signs like *Ye Olde Redde Bulle*, with the pronunciation properly /ði/ not /ji/.

It is with the coming of Christianity that the continuous history of English orthography begins. The written word was an important adjunct of the spread of the Word of God, for from early in its history the church had relied heavily on the written testimony of those who had had living contact with God on earth. The ultimate success of the English conversion rested in large measure on the instruction of native

---

[1] The limits of the linguistic periods, Old, Middle and Modern English, are defined in the Abbreviations on p. viii.

[2] Latin ⟨th⟩ had always been recognised as an alternative to thorn by English writers; even before the Norman Conquest, foreign names were spelt with either: *Elizabeth* or *Elizabeþ*, *Thomas* or *þomas*.

[3] The ascender of ⟨þ⟩ had become so reduced by the fifteenth century that the graph looked rather like a reversed ⟨y⟩ in the manuscripts (see, for example, plate 5); in some manuscripts, indeed, the two forms were identical (e.g. plate 2).

young men in the ministry, to continue the work of the foreign missionaries, and instruction involved knowledge of the Bible and use of service books. Thus the spread of education in reading and writing may be seen as the keystone of the conversion. However, writing was not to prove of interest to the ecclesiastical orders alone, for it seems that the missionaries were not slow to make clear the church's potential usefulness in secular administration. An important date in the conversion of the Anglo-Saxons is 597 when a mission from Pope Gregory the Great, headed by Augustine, landed in Kent. In some senses the pope's authority represented a continuation of that of the Roman emperor, and the early church had learnt from its imperial predecessor the value of an efficient organisation. In England this is seen in the church's immediate interest in the codification of law. A lawcode of Æðelberht of Kent, the first English monarch to be converted by the Roman missionaries, was committed to writing some time before his death in 616, not twenty years after Augustine's arrival, and the fact that no less than three Kentish lawcodes of the seventh century survive, albeit in copies of a much later date, indicates that legal writing was well established in that early period. Later identification of the church with the temporal government may be seen in the growth of the king's secretariat or writing-house, filled, until long after the Norman Conquest, with clerics. By the tenth century the secretariat (later called the chancery) was responsible for the day-to-day business of running the kingdom, for recording the king's acts and ordinances, and for finance. Thus although the teaching of writing was confined to the monasteries, and although the skill was not normally practised by the laity, the value and importance of writing were brought to the notice of a wide circle of powerful men in the land.

English Christianity has two roots, one in Rome and the other in Ireland, for Irish monks were settling in Northumbria at the time that Augustine landed in Kent. The script used in Old English manuscripts shows the importance of Irish teaching in the early years of the English conversion for it is a development of the Irish version of the roman alphabet. Irish Christianity was marked by monastic zeal and devotion to scholarship, and Anglo-Saxons everywhere took up both with an enthusiasm which made England in general and Northumbria in particular an intellectual centre of Europe by the end of the seventh century. The many well-stocked English libraries of the period were filled mainly with books imported from Gaul, but soon after the middle of the seventh century we find records of books produced in England being sent abroad, and by 735 when Bede, the most famous son of Northumbrian monasticism, died, the products of English scribes and scholarship were being exported in large numbers. Such products were, of course, in the church's international language, Latin, but it is recorded of Bede himself that he translated parts of the Gospels and other material into English, and it is in the margin of two copies (both made within a year or two of Bede's death) of his most famous work, *Historia Ecclesiastica Gentis Anglorum,* that there appear the earliest surviving records of written English, nine lines by the first known English poet, Cædmon, whose life Bede tells in the *Historia.*

The history of written English begins with seventh-century lawcodes and the translations into the vernacular made by Bede, but the latter have not survived and the former are extant only in twelfth-century copies the spelling of which has been modernised. Consequently our knowledge of the early history of our orthography stems from a slightly later period. Marginal and interlinear entries in English (such as the Cædmon poem) appear in a few eighth-century Latin manuscripts; and in the ninth century, legal documents in English and continuous inter-linear glosses are more numerous. But it is only from the time of King Alfred (died 899) that records are sufficiently full for us to trace the history of spelling in detail.

Alfred, perhaps the best known of early English kings, was not king of England but of Wessex. In the centuries after the Anglo-Saxon migration to Britain, numerous small kingdoms appeared in what is now England. Gradually the stronger absorbed the weaker until at the end of the eighth century only three dominant ones were left: Northumbria, extending from the Humber estuary to the Firth of Forth in the east, with a slightly less secure hold on a comparable area of the west; Mercia, the kingdom of the midlands; and Wessex, the area ruled by the West Saxons, south of the Thames. During the ninth century, Danish vikings attacking from the east subjugated Northumbria and Mercia, and at the end of the century Alfred fought a rear-guard action in Wessex, an action which was ultimately successful and which confined Danish settlement and rule to the east and north of a line extending roughly from London to Derby. In the tenth century, Alfred's successors conquered the Danish areas and established the boundaries of England approximately where they stand today. Thus England was unified under the West Saxon royal house.

Map 1

English kingdoms in the ninth century, showing towns mentioned in the text.

Our knowledge of the spoken dialects of Anglo-Saxon England is not unnaturally slender, but the Humber and the Thames have probably always been important dialect boundaries, and it seems reasonable to assume that regional dialect speech coincided to some extent with political units in Anglo-Saxon times. In the somewhat scanty written records of English up to the tenth century, linguistic historians recognise four 'dialects', Northumbrian, Mercian, Kentish and West Saxon, by which they mean varieties of written language associated with four geographical regions, distinguished by the use of different spelling conventions and to a lesser extent different accidence, vocabulary and syntax. The spelling systems of the four dialects are sufficiently distinct to be readily detected, but it should not be supposed that there appears within each consistency of the order of that pertaining in Modern English, although, as will be seen below, by the end of the tenth century a stable system not unlike our own was widely used. Indeed, with the exception of West Saxon, the dialects are fairly sparsely recorded. Northumbrian appears in early fragments and a few isolated texts of the tenth century; Kentish is discernible in scattered remains throughout the period, but usually only in conjunction with traits of other dialects; and Mercian appears in a pure form in one notable text of the ninth century (the Vespasian Psalter gloss) and in a number of items of the tenth century which have varying degrees of West Saxon influence, dependent on their date and place of composition. Though the origin of the different systems is regional, their prominence and use are related primarily to political considerations. For example, the spelling in use in Canterbury, the primary archbishopric, though it contains distinctive Kentish features throughout Old English times, also contains evidence of external influence. In the ninth century, the long political dominance over southern England of Mercian kings (and the consequent appointment of Mercians to the Canterbury see) produced in Kentish documents a variety of the Mercian spelling system in which occasional lapses into Kentish may be observed. But during the ninth century the political influence of Mercia declined and that of Wessex grew. Ninth-century West Saxon texts, including writings of the reign of King Alfred at the end of that century, show, like contemporary Kentish texts, a noticeable dependence on the Mercian spelling system, but gradually a distinctive West Saxon 'house-style' stabilised until towards the end of the tenth century it in turn had become the universal standard, affecting the writings of pre-Conquest tradition ensured a positive element of continuity of English spelling, at least in the south and west, from the tenth century until a renewed movement towards stabilisation began in the fourteenth. The roman alphabet used in the West Saxon tradition was largely that which we use today, the letters being adopted with the sound value associated with them in medieval Latin. But there are differences between tenth- and twentieth-century usage. ⟨j v w⟩ did not then form part of the roman alphabet, and the Anglo-Saxons usually avoided ⟨q⟩ and ⟨z⟩. They had, on the other hand, four extra letters: the vowel ligature ⟨æ⟩, derived from Latin and representing the vowel of Modern English *ash* (which is its Old English name); crossed ⟨d⟩ known as eth (⟨ð⟩), derived from Irish to represent, alongside the runic thorn (cf. p. 2), both voiced and voiceless dental fricatives; and two symbols from the runic alphabet, thorn and a character called wynn (representing /w/), similar in form to thorn but lacking an ascender (cf. plate 1). None of these except thorn survived beyond the thirteenth century, ⟨æ⟩ generally becoming written ⟨a⟩, eth being replaced by thorn or ⟨th⟩ because it was liable to confusion with ⟨d⟩, and wynn being dropped in favour of a doubled ⟨u⟩ or ⟨v⟩ which ultimately became invariably linked in our modern ⟨w⟩.[1] Occasionally ⟨q⟩ and ⟨z⟩ were used before the Norman Conquest in foreign names or technical words, e.g. *reliquias* 'relics', a learned borrowing from Latin, or *Elizabeth*. Since the two graphemes were in more widespread use in French, the flood of Romance loanwords which accompanied the French invasion after 1066 familiarised English writers with them. But ⟨z⟩ has always had to fight ⟨s⟩ for its existence in English (cf. 'Thou whoreson zed, thou unnecessary letter!' *King Lear* II. ii. 68), and remains one of the least used members of our alphabet. ⟨q⟩ had greater success, for the French combination ⟨qu⟩ spread into the comparatively few English words with the group /kw/ and eventually replaced the native ⟨cw⟩ completely, Old English *cwen* and *cwic* becoming Modern English *queen* and *quick*.[2]

[1] Modern editors of Old English texts usually supply ⟨w⟩ for manuscript wynn, just as they replace the various manuscript forms of ⟨s⟩ (e.g. ⟨ʃ⟩) with ⟨s⟩. But ⟨æ þ ð⟩ are retained because any departure would be to supply two modern characters for a single early one, or to falsify equally radically in some other way. Most modern editions also print ⟨g⟩ for the 'open' character of Old English script, but in this history an indication of the manuscript form will be retained (⟨ȝ⟩) for reasons which will become clear in chapter 2.

[2] The establishment of ⟨qu⟩ was greatly facilitated by scribes' knowledge of it in Latin. The earliest Old English texts use it occasionally rather than ⟨cw⟩ even in native words.

Canterbury scribes, of those in the old Mercian kingdom, and even (in the eleventh century) of those working north of the Humber. In other words, the tenth-century change in Canterbury from the Mercian standard to the West Saxon one was induced by political changes. We shall see later how other important political changes affected the development of spelling.

What has come to be known as the West Saxon scribal tradition produced in the late Old English period a remarkably rigid spelling system in use throughout England. The success of the scribal tradition in stabilising spelling cannot be overstressed. It came about at a time when the political situation was particularly favourable, for under the reign of Edgar (959–75) the country was united, prosperous and free from external attack. During this time too a reform of the Benedictine order, instigated in the south, revitalised monastic life throughout England; repopulation of old monasteries and the creation of many new ones caused a sudden heavy demand for books, particularly in the vernacular, and scribal activity reached a peak in the closing years of the millennium. The very use of the vernacular on such a wide scale is in itself remarkable, unparalleled elsewhere in Europe at this date. It had been an English tradition from the time of Bede, but it was given stimulus and authority in the last decade of Alfred's reign when the king himself instigated a series of translations from Latin for the benefit of a people intellectually impoverished by ruinous invasions of the vikings in the ninth century. The stabilisation of spelling was facilitated by the fact that English had become widely used in book production just when large numbers of books were being produced. By the end of the tenth century, the speed at which books had to be copied, the new firm control exercised over the enclosed orders (the producers of books), the fact that most if not all surviving writings are the products of professional scribes, and the new political unity of England all helped to create a single stable orthography for English, and this was to have profound effects on the history of spelling.

During the first half of the eleventh century, writing throughout England conformed to the West Saxon standard, and the many books which survive from the period (their numbers run into three figures) give little internal clue about whether they were written in Exeter, Canterbury, Worcester or York. Though later centuries saw the breakdown of standardisation consequent upon the political upheaval after the Norman Conquest, the firm foundation offered by this

2

Plate 1

Ælfric, *Homily on the Lord's Prayer*, Cambridge University Library MS Gg 3 28 (circa 1000) fol. 56v lower half. Passage i (p. 9) begins nine lines from the bottom.

The writings of Abbot Ælfric, the most accomplished prose writer of the period, exemplify late Old English spelling very well. Ælfric was trained at Winchester, in the heart of Wessex, in the time of Bishop Æðelwold, one of the architects of the Benedictine reform referred to above, and the scribes employed on the best manuscripts of his works are faithful to his West Saxon language. His rendering of the Lord's Prayer which follows was made about the year 990, and a number of near contemporary copies of it survive, one of them in a manuscript annotated by the author himself.[1] In none does the spelling vary at all significantly from that printed here. (This version is taken from the manuscript illustrated in plate 1, Cambridge University Library MS Gg 3 28.)[2]

i.

Þu ure fæder, þe eart on heofonum, sy þin nama ȝehalȝod. Cume ðin rice. Sy ðin wylla on eorðan swaswa on heofonum. Syle us todæȝ urne dæȝhwamlican hlaf. And forȝyf us ure ȝyltas swaswa we forȝyfað ðamþe wið us aȝyltað. And ne læd ðu na us on costnunȝe, ac alys us fram yfele.[3]

The majestic simplicity of this prose, equal to that of the King James version, is brought out by comparison with a separate translation of the same passage copied a generation or two later in Bath Abbey.[4] A heavier dependence on Latin is noticeable in the second version in word-order (*Fæder ure* for *Pater noster*) and word-building (*to-becume* for

[1] British Museum MS Royal 7 C xii.

[2] The following is an approximation of the pronunciation of this passage at the time of (or soon after) its copying circa 1000:

/θu: u:rə 'fædər θe ært ān 'hevənən 'si: θi:n 'nāmə je'hɑ:lyəd 'kumə θi:n 'ri:tʃə 'si: θi:n 'wilə ān 'e:rðən swaswa ān 'hevənən 'sylə u:s to 'dæɪ u:rnə 'dæɪʍāmlitʃən 'lɑ:f ān(d) for'jif u:s u:rə 'gyltəs swaswa we: for'jivəθ θāmθe wið u:s a'gyltəθ ān(d) nə læ:d θu: 'na: u:s ān 'kostnuŋgə ak a'li:s u:s frām 'yvələ/

The pronunciation of ten centuries ago is naturally dubious. Some of the controversial points in this transcription, such as the pronunciation of ⟨i⟩ and ⟨y⟩ are discussed below. Not all of the sounds indicated here are of phonemic status. Probably [ā, v, ð, ŋ, ɣ] are not but their inclusion gives a modern reader a clearer impression of the actual pronunciation.

[3] There are few abbreviations in Old English manuscripts compared with contemporary Latin writings. Two of the commonest, a tilde or wavy mark above a vowel signifying a following ⟨m⟩, and a large 7-like character for *and* (actually a reduced form of Latin *et*), are expanded silently in this passage and the next.

[4] The scriptorium in which passage i was copied cannot be identified with certainty. Ælfric composed the homily in which the translation appears in the monastery of Cernel (now Cerne Abbas), Dorset, but this particular copy belonged for most of the Middle Ages to Durham Cathedral Priory.

ad-veniat), but differences in spelling from the Ælfric passage, indicated here by heavy type, are very slight indeed.

ii.
Fæder ure, þu þe eart on heofonum, si þin nama ʒehalʒod. Tobecume þin rice. ʒewurþe ðin willa on eorðan swaswa on heofonum. Urne ʒedæʒhwamlican hlaf syle us todæʒ. And forʒyf us ure ʒyltas swaswa we forʒyfað urum ʒyltendum. And ne ʒelæd þu us on costnunʒe, ac alys us of yfele.[1]

Comparison of the two passages, independently composed and copied by scribes at different centres, with a time gap of perhaps a quarter of a century, reveals just how stable late Old English spelling was. Consistency of spelling is maintained in individual words, with only two exceptions: ⟨þ⟩ and ⟨ð⟩ are interchangeable graphs, both being employed in the same word by both scribes (*þin*, *ðin*, Mod. E *thy*, *thine*), and ⟨i⟩ and ⟨y⟩ are interchangeable vowel graphs, the scribe of passage i preferring the latter (*sy*, *wylla*) and that of ii employing ⟨i⟩ (*si*, *willa*). From the standpoint of Modern English, which has two dental fricative phonemes, /θ/ and /ð/, it seems remarkable that Old English scribes did not use their two symbols to mark the distinction, their failure to do so being the root cause of our representation of the two phonemes in current English by the single grapheme ⟨th⟩.[2] But at the time that ⟨þ⟩ came into use alongside ⟨ð⟩, the two sounds [θ] and [ð] were sub-phonemic, i.e. the sounds were varied according to context (cf. Mod. E *teeth*, *teething*) and were not meaningfully distinct. As the pronunciation could be inferred from the context, two graphemes were not needed. The growth in popularity of ⟨þ⟩, adopted much later than ⟨ð⟩, is probably to be explained, like its longer survival, by the fact that confusion with similarly shaped graphs was less likely. The interchangeability of ⟨i⟩ and ⟨y⟩ is partly the product of Latin influence, for the two were variants in medieval Latin, and partly is caused by phonemic change, for by the end of the tenth century there are signs that the phonemes represented by the two symbols, earlier separate, had fallen together in most dialects, and it is from that period that many scribes used ⟨i⟩ and ⟨y⟩ indiscriminately. In some areas and by some scribes there were attempts at systematisation, for example many manuscripts show use of ⟨i⟩ particularly in the neigh-

[1] From Corpus Christi College, Cambridge, MS 140.
[2] ⟨th⟩ may be considered a grapheme sequence rather than a grapheme but the distinction is not relevant here. The term grapheme is similarly 'loosely' used throughout this book.

bourhood of symbols representing palatal consonants ⟨c g h⟩, but this was a short-lived and never entirely successful discrimination. By the end of the Old English period, ⟨i⟩ and ⟨y⟩ had become alternative symbols for the same vowel and remained so until comparatively recent times.[1] The stability of late West Saxon orthography may be stressed by comparison with a gloss to the Lord's Prayer made in Northumbria half a century earlier (the gloss to the famous Lindisfarne Gospels).

iii.
Fader urer ðu arð in heofnum, sie ӡehalӡud noma ðin. Tocymeð ric ðin. Sie willo ðin suæ is in heofne ond in eorðo. Hlaf userne ofer wistlic sel us todæӡ. Ond forӡef us scylda usra suæ uoe forӡefon scyldӡum usum. Ond ne inlæd usih in costunӡe, ah ӡefriӡ usich from yfle.

Among the numerous differences between this and the West Saxon passages may be pointed out *suæ, ond, uoe, ah* and *from* against West Saxon *swa, and, we, ac, fram*. These are purely orthographic differences which do not reflect different regional pronunciations,[2] and they illustrate the existence of at least one other quite distinct orthography in tenth-century England. But no spelling system other than the West Saxon one became so widespread or was itself used with such consistency. Even within this short passage the Northumbrian scribe shows some variation in the spelling of individual words (inflectional endings in parenthesis): *urer, user(ne), us(um)*; and *usih, usich*.

As a whole, Old English spelling as developed in the West Saxon tradition was much nearer a one-to-one relationship with sounds than is its Modern English descendant.[3] More consonants represented a

[1] Even today a few words containing them are not fixed (*gipsy, gypsy; pigmy, pygmy; siren, syren; tiro, tyro*), while our present practice of preferring ⟨y⟩ finally and ⟨i⟩ internally results in such pairs as *happy, happier; day, daily*. Shades of earlier confusion remain in *dryness* (cf. *happiness* or *drier*), *shyness, shyly*, etc.

[2] Until the appearance in the sixteenth century of writers who make specific statements about the pronunciation of their own day, regional differences of pronunciation are difficult to determine, but inference may be drawn from careful examination of the use of the alphabet in each scribal tradition when knowledge of the general history of the language and the dialectal variations of more recent English are borne in mind. From such information it is possible to say that the Northumbrian ⟨e⟩ spelling in *forӡef* does indicate a quite different vowel position from West Saxon ⟨y⟩ in *forӡyf* whereas those listed in the text do not.

[3] The sources of our knowledge of the sounds of Early English are beyond the scope of this book to examine in detail, though some comments on them are made incidentally in this chapter and the next. Briefly, we have a reasonably full understanding of phonemic distinctions in Old English, but phonetic values are more difficult to determine.

single phoneme invariably than they do in Modern English (some discrepancies which developed by the end of the period being considered in chapter 3), and there were none of the 'silent' consonants which appear comparatively frequently in the current system. Vowels too were much more simply denoted than in Modern English, each vowel grapheme equating with one vowel position. Vowel length, however, was not normally indicated, the short vowel /i/ in *timber* 'timber', for example, being identical in written form with the long vowel /i:/ in *tima* 'time'.[1] The widespread use of a single stable spelling system for an extended period meant that accuracy of phonemic representation was increasingly disturbed in the eleventh century, and spellings which had had one-to-one relationship with sounds gradually lost it as the phonemic pattern altered. For example, the common vowel graphemes ⟨ea⟩ and ⟨eo⟩ represented monophthongs by the time of the Norman Conquest, falling together, in some areas, with sounds represented ⟨æ⟩ and ⟨e⟩,[2] while simplification of double consonants in speech led to considerable laxity in the doubling of consonant graphemes (a feature which aided the rise of the doubled consonant as an indicator of a preceding short vowel in later centuries, cf. p. 50). Vowels in unstressed syllables gradually fell together in /ə/, so that in passage i, for example, the symbols ⟨e a o⟩ all represent the same unstressed vowel; eleventh-century scribes frequently confused these graphemes (and also ⟨u⟩) in inflectional endings and affixes.[3] Phonological change involving consonant groups resulted in the matching of digraphs with single phonemes: because the group /sk/ became simplified to /ʃ/, the sequence ⟨sc⟩ came to represent this single phoneme (e.g. *scip* 'ship', with a pronunciation as in Modern

---

[1] Acute accents and doubling of the vowel symbol are two methods occasionally used to indicate long vowels, especially in monosyllabic words when homographs might otherwise confuse a reader (e.g. *god* 'God', *gód* 'good' (or, substantively, 'goodness'), *man* 'man', *mán* 'crime').

[2] There has been considerable disagreement amongst Old English scholars over the question of the realisation of vowel grapheme sequences. It seems reasonable to suppose that when such graphemes as ⟨ea⟩ and ⟨eo⟩ appear as reflexes of Common Germanic diphthongs, they themselves represent diphthongs, but a difficulty arises in the case of the same graphemes appearing as the reflexes of Common Germanic monophthongs, especially when the subsequent history of English shows them to be monophthongs later also. Cf. C. Sprockel, *The Language of the Parker Chronicle*, vol. I Phonology and Accidence, The Hague 1965, pp. 129 ff. and references.

[3] Confusion of unstressed vowels is already to be observed in tenth-century Northumbrian, and may be seen in passage iii (e.g. *ȝehalȝud, willo* compared with West Saxon *ȝehalȝod, willa*).

English), and because the initial combination /xw/ became the simple voiceless consonant /ʍ/, the sequence ⟨hw⟩ represented /ʍ/ just as ⟨wh⟩ frequently does in Modern English (cf. OE *hwit*, Mod. E *white*).[1] Eleventh-century English spelling, then, was not an accurate phonemic transcription, but, except as regards a limited range of 'permitted' variants (e.g. in the doubling of consonants or the representation of unstressed vowels), the tradition that each lexical item should be spelt in a set manner was already strong. This is the point made most forcibly by comparison of passages i and ii.

How long that tradition lasted may be assessed by examination of a fourth Lord's Prayer translation, this taken from the end of a Psalter copied at Shaftesbury circa 1100.[2] Like passage iii, this is a gloss on Latin, but the translation is quite independent of all those so far quoted. Instances of orthographic changes which have taken place in the hundred years since the copying of passage i are shown by the use of heavy type.

iv.
Fæder ure, þu ðe eart on heou**e**num, si gehalgod nama þin. To-becume rice þin. Gewyrþe willa þin swa on heou**e**num and on eorþan. [Hlaf] urne dæihwamlice syle us todæ**i**. And forgif us gyltas ure easwa and we forgiuan gyltendrum urum. And na us ingelæd on costnigna, ac alys us fram yuele.

Only one of these changes indicates an alteration in the phonemic structure: earlier *dæȝ* has become *dæi* because of the vocalisation of the palatal fricative represented by ⟨ȝ⟩ and the formation of a diphthong not unlike that which survives in *day*.[3] The other change is for the moment an orthographic one, and is due to the influence of Latin practice: ⟨u⟩ has come to represent the voiced allophone of Old English /f/, although at this time it is unlikely that /f/ had split into /f/ and /v/.[4]

---

[1] Likewise ⟨hl, hn, hr⟩ represented /l̥, n̥, r̥/, developed from /xl, xn, xr/. Cf. p. 47 and footnote. The one instance of a single symbol representing a consonantal combination is ⟨x⟩ for /ks/, but the combination might also be written ⟨cs⟩ or ⟨hs⟩: *axian, acsian, ahsian*.

[2] From the Salisbury Psalter, Salisbury Cathedral MS 150. On the use of ⟨g⟩ rather than ⟨ȝ⟩, cf. p. 22.

[3] The vocalisation probably occurred some time earlier. Spelling is only one of many sorts of evidence used in determining when a sound-change took place, and it is usually safe to suppose that changes in spelling appear only after a considerable time lag.

[4] The sub-phonemic distinction of [θ] and [ð] referred to above is paralleled by that of other fricatives: [s] and [z] were not separate phonemes in Old English either, the voiced sound appearing only between other voiced sounds, and this is the reason that we still use the same grapheme for what are now separate phonemes in *house*,

Passage iv shows how marginal were the orthographic developments of the eleventh century. Of even greater significance is the fact that such changes were not at all indicative of the area or scriptorium in which this gloss was written, for the spelling as a whole still follows the universal standard. The existence of a stable spelling tradition at a very early date is of great importance in the development of English orthography. In the first place, it has meant that some of the conventions of contemporary English spelling have a very long history. Those mentioned already include the marginal overlapping of ⟨i⟩ and ⟨y⟩, the lack of separate graphemes to equate with /ð/ and /θ/, and the use of ⟨s⟩ for /z/, while the development of the use of double consonants to indicate vowel length and the popularity of such a vowel grapheme as ⟨ea⟩ are discussed in chapter 3 below. But the repercussions of early stabilisation are perhaps even wider, for one is probably justified in seeing it at the very root of all our present orthographic troubles. Though, in later centuries, English spelling was considerably influenced by the conventions of foreign systems, particularly those of French, the native tradition was never entirely lost, and our spelling is thus the result of the overlaying, for nearly a thousand years, of one tradition upon another. The following chapters will attempt to trace on the one hand the slow and painful redevelopment of a universally accepted orthography after the disturbance of the Old English uniformity consequent upon the French invasion, and on the other the sequence of events which has caused us to erect such a curious and at times eccentric building on so simple and sound a ground-plan.

houses /haʊs, haʊzɪz/; cf. the dental fricative parallel in *truth, truths* /truːθ, truːðz/, rarely /truːθs/. With the labio-dental fricatives the case is slightly different, for although [f] and [v] were similarly subphonemic in Old English, literary borrowings from Latin gave rise to changes in late Old English orthography. In early borrowings into Old English, Latin ⟨v⟩ was expressed as ⟨f⟩ (e.g. *efa* 'Eve'); in the case of words which reached the spoken language, Latin /v/ in a position in which the voiced sound was not found in Old English (e.g. initially) was unvoiced. Hence Modern English *fan*, borrowed as *fann* in Old English, is from Latin *vannus*. But in the late Old English period, familiarity of scribes with written Latin caused eleventh-century literary borrowings such as Latin *versus* to appear with either the native ⟨f⟩ or with Latin ⟨v⟩, *fers* or *vers*, and though *fers* persisted until the fourteenth century, it is the form closer to the Latin which has survived (Mod. E *verse*). Since scribes became used to ⟨v⟩ to represent Latin /v/, they tended occasionally to extend it to native words containing [v] medially, and with the arrival in subsequent centuries of many French loanwords with /v/ initially, so that voiced and voiceless sounds became phonemic, /v/ and /f/ came to be distinguished regularly graphemically. (N.B. it should be added that ⟨u⟩ and ⟨v⟩ were never distinguished in Latin and not in English until the seventeenth century (cf. p. 81), so that ⟨v⟩ in this footnote encompasses both ⟨v⟩ and ⟨u⟩.)

Chapter 2   The collapse of the standard

On the evening of 14 October 1066, King Harold II's standard fell beneath a charge of Norman knights at a hundred boundary marked by an old apple tree some seven miles from Hastings. For almost a century after the death of the last representative of England's political domination by Wessex, the West Saxon spelling standard continued to be adhered to over most of the country, but eventually it too succumbed, and the disruption of the orthography and the proliferation of regional spelling habits in the Middle English period must be seen as direct results of the social upheaval which William I's victory prefaced.

In the years following the Norman Conquest large numbers of French-speaking settlers were established in England, and for some two centuries the country had two living languages. During the civil disturbances which plagued William's twenty-year reign, most of the native aristocracy were killed, outlawed, or ousted from positions of authority. French became the language of the ruling class, and remained important as the court language and the medium of parliament and the law until the fourteenth century. The unique position of English as the only vernacular of Europe extensively used in official documents and with a fully developed standard literary form was lost not because the conquerors held the native language in any sort of disrespect but because they had no use for it. Their numbers were sufficient for their own language to be maintained, to be passed on to succeeding generations, and to be learnt by native English speakers because of the social prestige it attracted.

The decline of a universal spelling system in early Middle English was the result essentially of a considerable reduction in the output of material in English. The abandoning of English in official writings was necessitated by the fact that those for whom such material was intended, the executive arm of the state, could neither speak nor read the language. A decline in the secular demand for books also followed the change of dynasty. There were probably fewer lay patrons of monastic scriptoria immediately after the Conquest, literacy amongst the Norman aristocracy being less widespread than it was in late Anglo-Saxon England, and those Normans who were interested in acquiring books required them to be in French or in Latin. Furthermore, spiritual as well as temporal power passed into different hands in post-Conquest England. Rome had supported William's invasion in return for a promise of reform of the English church on lines approved by the papacy, and many French-speaking clerics, headed by the redoubtable scholar Lanfranc (Archbishop of Canterbury 1070–88), were given important ecclesiastical positions in England. The English church of the early eleventh century had already begun to outgrow the emphasis on the vernacular which had been so useful in revitalising scholarship after the doldrums of the ninth century, and Latin learning was once again important. But the example of King Alfred's translations and the success of Abbot Ælfric in vernacular composition (see chapter 1) ensured the continuing popularity and authority of English, at least until the effects of the Conquest were widely felt. However, by the twelfth century the new bishops and abbots from France encouraged the filling of monastic libraries with books in Latin, and the masters of the scriptoria, also often French-speaking and trained in the continental tradition, were hardly able to foster the native vernacular. Gradually the number of scribes engaged in the copying of English writings declined, and the careful training of novices in conventional spelling, so important in the maintenance of a universal orthography, was neglected.

Comparatively little written English survives from the two centuries from 1100 to 1300, and it is difficult to trace the continuous development in that period of a single orthography or to follow the practices of an individual scriptorium. But occasionally chance events have given us special opportunities. At Peterborough, for example, the library was lost in a disastrous fire which swept through the monastery in 1116. By 1121 it was rebuilt, and stocked by the usual practice of borrowing books from elsewhere and copying them. One of the volumes which has survived from the restocking is a version of the *Anglo-Saxon Chronicle*, an annalistic account in English of events of national and local importance, created in the time of King Alfred and continued at many of the larger monastic centres throughout the tenth and eleventh centuries. The copying of the *Chronicle* does not necessarily indicate a special interest in history in the Peterborough monks, for historical documents of all kinds were preserved for their possible usefulness in the litigation over rights to land in which abbeys frequently found themselves in the Middle Ages, but whatever the reason behind the copying, the creation of the book seems to have given new impetus to chronicle writing. Additional entries in English were made on four occasions up to 1132, and a final long section was added to cover the period up to 1154. Thus in the *Peterborough Chronicle* we have a series of dated writings spanning the first half of the twelfth century. In them, strict conformity to late Old English accidence is increasingly lost, as is the ability to reproduce the control of the written medium displayed by eleventh-century annalists. In spelling, at first the West Saxon standard (as it had developed by 1100) was well maintained, but gradually the scribes' lack of training reveals itself, until the final entry shows only an imperfect grasp of the orthography.[1]

The situation at Peterborough is perhaps typical of what happened throughout England in the twelfth century, though the decline did not take place everywhere at the same pace, for at some centres, particularly in the south and west, links with the earlier tradition were much stronger. The important point is that while orthographic developments, both those induced by sound-changes and those which came about by imitation of conventions in other languages, took place much as they had done in the eleventh century (cf. p. 13), they were no longer national developments, and this constitutes the major distinction between the Old and Middle English periods. Possibly feudalism was in part responsible. Though during the last decades of the Anglo-Saxon administration a semi-feudal structure had already emerged in society, it was only under Henry I (1100–35) that the full effects of the introduction of the system as it is generally understood today were felt. In particular, movement of people about the country was limited and regionalism consequently encouraged. But this can be only part of the story. Of more importance is the fact that once English ceased to be used by those in authority, either in secular administrative documents issued by central government or in prestigious ecclesiastical writings, there was no national standard to follow. In areas in which

[1] Confusion is shown in the gradual infiltration of Latin conventions, e.g. ⟨ch⟩ for /x/, ⟨th⟩ for /θ/, ⟨u⟩ or ⟨uu⟩ for /w/. Worst of all was the effect on vowel graphemes. In Latin ⟨æ⟩ and ⟨e⟩ had fallen together, while in English ⟨æ⟩, ⟨ea⟩ and ⟨a⟩ had done so. Peterborough scribes confused all four.

Figure 1

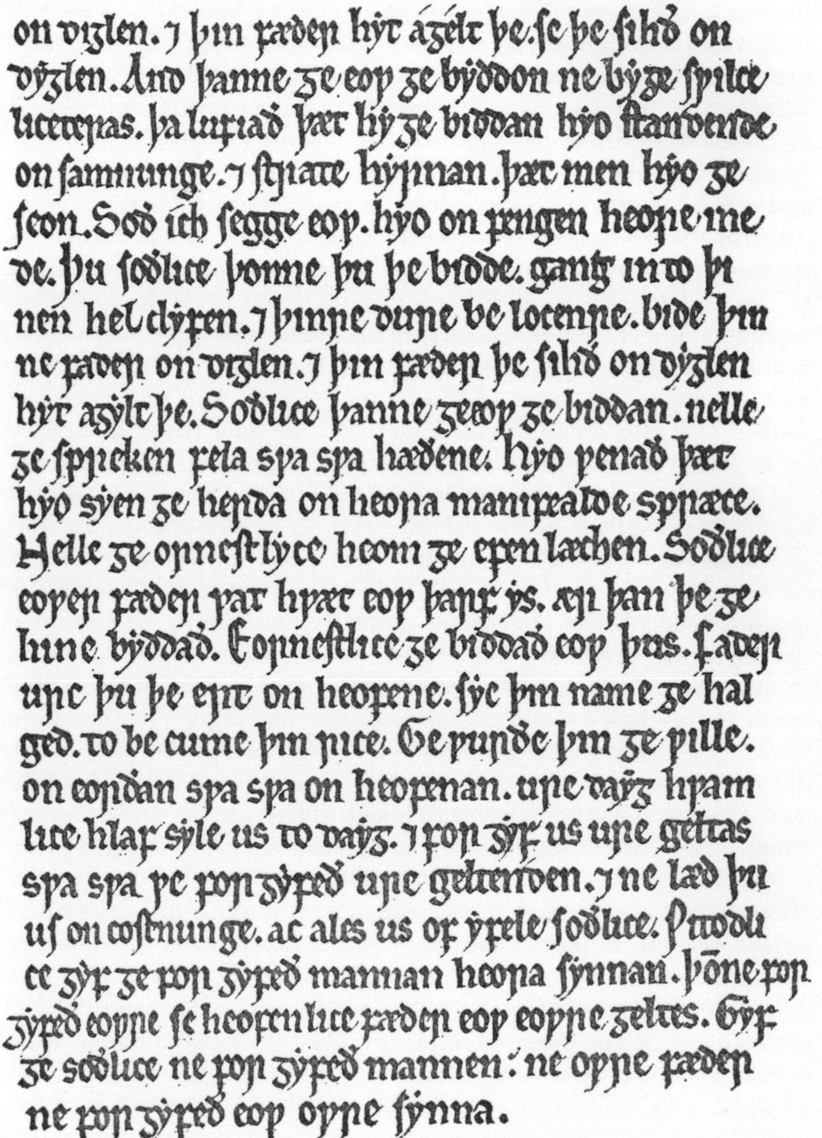

on wizlen. ꝼ þin ꞃæden hyr ᴀᵹelr þe.ſe þe ſihð on
wizlen. Anð þanne ᵹe eop ᵹe byðdon ne byᵹe ſpilce
liceꞃpas. þa luꝼiað þær hyᵹe biðdan hyo ſtanðenðe
on ſamnunge. ꝼ ſpiace hyꝺnan. þær men hyo ᵹe
ſcon. Soð ich ſegge eop. hyo on þingen heoꝼie me
ve. þu ſoðlice þonne þu þe biðde. gang in to þi
nen hel clyꝼen. ꝼ þinne vuꞃe be locenꝺe. biðe þin
ne ꞃaðen on wizlen. ꝼ þin ꞃæðen þe ſihð on wizlen
hyr aᵹylr þe. Soðlice þanne ᵹeop ᵹe biddan. nelle
ᵹe ſpꞃieken ꞃela ſpa ſpa hæðene. hyo penað þær
hyo ſyen ᵹe heꞃða on heoꞃa maniꞃxalðe ſppæce.
Nelle ᵹe opneſtlyec heom ᵹe epen læchen. Soðlice
eoꝺeꝺ ꞃaðeꝺ ꝺar hꝩær eop þanꝺ ys. æꝺ þan þe ᵹe
hine byððað. Eopneſtlice ᵹe biððað eop þus. Faðeꝺ
uꝺe þu þe eꝺr on heoꝼene. ſyc þin name ᵹe hal
ged. to be cume þin ꝺice. Ge puꝺðe þin ᵹe pille.
on coꝺðan ſpa ſpa on heoꝼenan. uꝺe vaꝩᵹ hꝩam
lice hlaꝼ ſyle us to vaꝩᵹ. ꝼ ꝼoꝺ ᵹyꝼ us uꝺe geltas
ſpa ſpa ꝺe ꝼoꝺ ᵹyꝼeð uꝺe gelrenðen. ꝼ ne læð þu
uſ on coſtnunge. ac ales us oꝼ yꝼele ſoðlice. Fꞃoðlu
ce ᵹyꝼ ᵹe ꝼoꝺ ᵹyꝼeð mannan heoꞃa ſyꝺnan. þone ꝼoꝺ
ᵹyꝼeð eoꝺꝺe ſe heoꝼen lice ꝼaðeꝺ eop eoꝺꝺe ᵹelras. Gyꝼ
ᵹe ſoðlice ne ꝼoꝺ ᵹyꝼeð mannen: ne oꝺꝺe ꞃaðeꝺ
ne ꝼoꝺ ᵹyꝼeð eop oꝺꝺe ſynna.

The West Saxon version of the Gospels, Bodleian Library MS Hatton 38 (circa 1200) fol. 85v. Passage v begins at the end of line 14.

strong continuity with Old English literary traditions was preserved, a stable spelling survived also. But such continuity became a localised affair, and regional differences in spelling, which were kept to a minimum in the eleventh century, gradually increased.

A useful example is provided by writings at Canterbury, where continuity throughout the Middle Ages was assured by the enduring importance of the see. The following extract is a copy made circa 1200 of the translation recorded in passage ii in chapter 1, with which it may usefully be compared.[1]

v.

Fader ure, þu þe ert on heofene, sye þin name ʒehalged. To-becume þin rice. Gewurðe þin ʒewille on eorðan swaswa on heofenan. Ure dayʒhwamlice hlaf syle us todayʒ. And forʒyf us ure geltas swaswa we forʒyfeð ure geltenden. And ne læd þu us on costnunge, ac ales us of yfele.

The passage should be seen in context. This particular translation occurs in the Old English version of the Gospels, and the very copying of such a text in its tenth-century translation as late as 1200 shows the veneration for that which is tested by time associated with Biblical texts. Hence the spelling is largely traditional, conforming for the most part to the West Saxon standard. The case can be made by examination of the form of the word *hlaf*, Mod. E *loaf*. The general history of the language as seen in its later development and as tested by contemporary spellings elsewhere shows that both the initial consonant group and the vowel had undergone phonological change in the centuries since the spelling was established. In early Old English, ⟨hl⟩ represented a consonant group /xl/, but by late Old English simplification to /l̥/ had taken place, and by 1200 the sound had almost everywhere been voiced to /l/. The vowel too, by 1200, had undergone some change from /ɑː/ to /ɔː/, the first stage of its movement towards modern /oʊ/. The spelling is thus traditional rather than phonetic. Nevertheless the spelling of the passage does record some linguistic developments, for example it shows in the reduction of many inflectional endings ⟨um⟩, ⟨a⟩, ⟨ne⟩, ⟨an⟩ to a uniform ⟨e⟩ that such inflections had been levelled to /ə/ (cf. p. 12). More importantly, the growth of regionalism in spelling is apparent in the three words *geltas*, *geltenden* and *ales*. If these are compared with the forms of the same words in passage ii (*ʒyltas*, *ʒyltendum*, *alys*), the Canterbury scribe of passage v may be seen

---

[1] Passage v is taken from Bodleian Library MS Hatton 38. The page on which it appears is reproduced opposite.

Map 2

Middle English dialect areas, showing towns mentioned in the text.

to be introducing ⟨e⟩ for earlier ⟨y⟩. This is an orthographic development which gives clear indication of the area of origin of the writing, for one of the simplest and most clearly marked traits of the more important regional orthographies in Middle English is the reflex of the close front rounded vowel which in early Old English appears as ⟨y⟩; broadly speaking, from the twelfth century the reflex in the north and east is ⟨i⟩ or ⟨y⟩ (which remain variant graphs of a single grapheme throughout Middle English, cf. p. 10), in the south-west ⟨u⟩, and in the south-east ⟨e⟩. Passage v may thus be identified on internal evidence as of south-eastern origin.

A few further observations on this tripartite development are of interest to the historian of English spelling. It is often extremely difficult for students of Early English to establish the relationship at any given period between the phonemic system of English (or a variety of English) and the graphemic system. In particular, it is not yet clear how closely the regional orthographies of Middle English reflect spoken dialects, though it is clear (and should be stressed) that the important regional spelling systems described in this book are traditional orthographies, having no closer relationship with speech sounds than any standardised and reasonably consistent spelling normally has. (In this sense they are not 'phonetic' systems.) They are also regional orthographies used over a wide geographical area which incorporated more than one regional variety of spoken English.[1] Nevertheless, some deductions about the spoken dialect which formed the basis of the written dialect may be made; for instance, the reflexes of Old English ⟨y⟩ suggest that /i/ and /y/ fell together in the north and east, but did not do so in some parts of the south-west, where scribes borrowed the French convention ⟨u⟩ for /y/ (cf. Mod. Fr. *tu, juste* /ty, ʒy:st/) to distinguish between this sound and /i/ (represented ⟨i⟩ or ⟨y⟩). Furthermore, in the south-east, where /i/ and /y/ also remained separate, /y/ fell in with /e/. It is clear too from a consideration of most words with Old English ⟨y⟩ which have survived to the present day that the spelling system of Modern English and contemporary Received Pronunciation are descendants of the north-eastern variety of Middle English (cf. p. 36), for ⟨i⟩ (/ɪ/) is the normal Modern English reflex (e.g. *king, sin*, OE *cyninʒ, synn*),[2] The other regional types have also

[1] For a detailed discussion of these points, see the articles by Professor Angus McIntosh cited in the bibliography.

[2] Cf. also *bride, mice* with long vowels, later diphthongised to /aɪ/ (OE *bryd, mys*), and the use of ⟨y⟩ in the final position: *dry* (OE *dryʒe*).

contributed marginally, Modern English having, for example, *knell*, *left*, *merry* from south-eastern orthography (OE *cnyll*, *lyft*, *myriȝ*) and *cudgel*, *crutch*, *dusty* (OE *cycȝel*, *crycc*, *dystiȝ*) from the south-west, with later falling together of /y/ and /ʌ/.[1] Sound and spelling from different varieties of Middle English have given us *bury* /berɪ/ (OE *byriȝean*) with western spelling and south-eastern pronunciation, and *busy* /bɪzɪ/ (OE *bysiȝ*) with western spelling and north-eastern pronunciation.

A quite different orthographic development observable in passage v is in the use of two varieties of the letter ⟨g⟩, used here and throughout Middle English as separate graphemes.[2] The insular script in which English is written up to the twelfth century had only an 'open' form of the letter: ⟨ȝ⟩. One of the more significant changes in scriptorium practice after the French took control is the abandoning of the insular script in favour of the carolingian (earlier used mainly in the copying of Latin), and our present 'closed' form ⟨g⟩ is the carolingian version of the letter. Although the insular script was in general discarded, scribes found it useful to preserve certain forms from it, for example the symbol ⟨þ⟩ discussed on page 2. Alongside carolingian ⟨g⟩[3] they retained ⟨ȝ⟩ (known as yogh)[4] to represent the second of the two phonemes /g/ and /j/ which were represented in late Old English by the single grapheme ⟨ȝ⟩. The distribution of the phonemes in late Old English was in part complementary,[5] but a serious overlap occurred in the initial position (cf. chapter 1, p. 9 and footnote 2: (*for*)ȝyf /-jif/ but ȝyltas /gyltəs/). Old English scribes made some attempt at distinction, representing /j/ by ⟨i⟩ when it occurred before a back vowel, or, if they used ⟨ȝ⟩, adding ⟨e⟩ between it and the vowel. Hence Modern English *yoke*, with a pronunciation in Old English /jo:k/, appeared as *ioc* or *ȝeoc*. But ambiguity remained before a front vowel. The two graphemes ⟨g⟩ and ⟨ȝ⟩ in Middle English improved matters, though

---

[1] N.B. /y/ has similarly become /ʌ/ in RP in French borrowings, e.g. *judge*, *just*, Mod. Fr. /ʒy:ʒ, ʒy:st/.

[2] The two letters can be seen clearly in figure 1 which incorporates the text of passage v. Note that this scribe has only one symbol for the upper case letter, hence *Gewurðe* rather than *ȝewurðe*.

[3] For typographical simplicity the carolingian symbol ⟨g⟩ will be represented by its modern printed equivalent ⟨g⟩.

[4] The name yogh (by which ⟨ȝ⟩ has been known since the fourteenth century) derives from the two graphemes which replaced it in late Middle English spelling: ⟨y⟩ initially and ⟨gh⟩ after a vowel.

[5] /g/ occurred usually before back vowels and consonants, /j/ normally only before and after front vowels.

Plate 2

yrken þi wt gode wille ·
and whils he saies hold ye stille ·
bot anspere at temptacionem
Set libera nos a malo amen ·
þrt were no nede ye yis to ken ·
for who con not yis are lewed men ·
when yis is done saye puerly ·
other prayer noune ý by ·
þat noþ first i laten
And sithen i englische als here is wryten ·
Fader oure þat is i heuen ·
blessid be þi name to neuen ·
come to vs þi kyngdome ·
In heuen & erthe þi wille be done ·
oure ilk day bred grunt vs to day ·
And oure mysdedes forgyue vs ay ·
als we do þpm yt trespasus
right so haue mercn vpon vs ·
and lede vs i no foundynge ·
bot shild vs fro al wicked þinge · amen ·
þen eft sone yo prest wil saye ·
stande stille & herken þi al waye
he saies Agnus thryse or he cese ·
yo last worde he spekis of þese ·
In ye yt þese may noght be ·
If you be oute of charyte ·
þen is gode of god to craue ·
þat you charyte may haue ·
þere when yo prest þar wil kis ·
knele you & pray þen yis ·

The Lay Folk's Mass Book, British Museum MS Royal 17 B xvii (fourteenth century) fol. 11r. Passage vii (p. 25) is the central section.

Plate 3

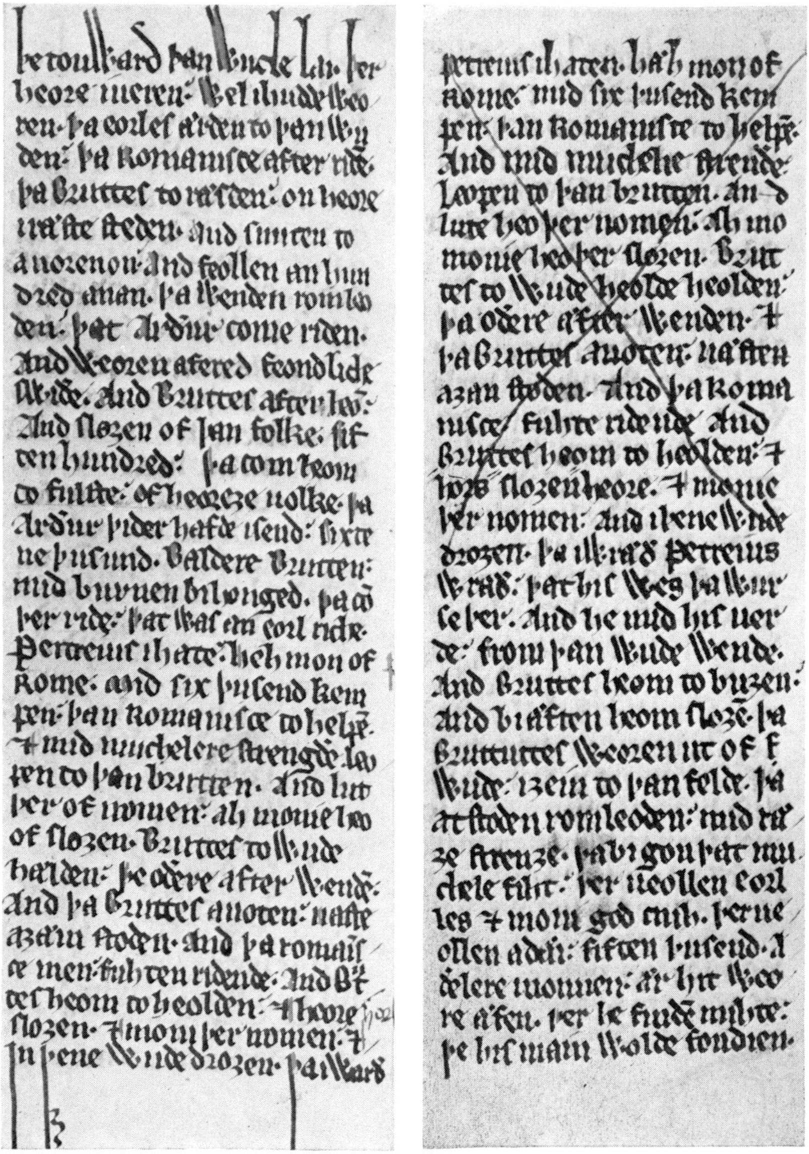

Laȝamon's *Brut*, British Museum MS Cotton Caligula A ix (thirteenth century) fol. 158v column 2 and fol. 159r column 1. The deleted section repeats the preceding fourteen lines of text.

⟨i⟩ (and its variant ⟨y⟩) continued to be used for /j/ also. With the arrival of printing, compositors in London, with no ⟨ʒ⟩ in their continental type, used ⟨i/y⟩ for /j/, and the second of these is preserved in modern spelling (e.g. *yoke*).[1] ⟨ʒ⟩ was also used in Middle English for the two allophones of /j/ which occurred after a vowel: [ç] and [x].[2] These two sounds gave scribes considerable difficulty in Middle English; among the many graphemes representing them are the Anglo-Norman ⟨s⟩, the Old English ⟨h⟩, the new grapheme ⟨ʒ⟩, and the last two combined as ⟨ʒh⟩. In the fifteenth century, when the distinction between ⟨ʒ⟩ and ⟨g⟩ became blurred, this combination was written ⟨gh⟩, and this is the sequence which has survived in a great many words in which [ç] and [x] were once heard, or still are in northern dialects, e.g. *high, ought, night, bough*.[3]

We have seen that to a limited extent (the use of ⟨e⟩ for earlier ⟨y⟩) regional spelling was in use in Canterbury by 1200. During the following two centuries, Kentish orthography became increasingly distinct from that used elsewhere, as can be seen from another translation of the Lord's Prayer, made in Canterbury in 1340:[4]

vi.
Vader oure, þet art ine heuenes, yhalʒed by þi name. Cominde þi riche. Yworþe þi wil ase ine heuene and ine erþe. Bread oure echedayes yef ous today. And uorlet ous oure yeldinges ase and we uorleteþ oure yelderes. And ne ous led naʒt into uondinge, ac vri ous uram queade.

In some ways this passage is further from Modern English than any of those so far cited, for example *vader* and *yef* look less like *father* and (*for*)*give* than do the *fader* and *forʒyf* of passage v, and this is entirely the result of the use of regional orthography. The most distinctive feature here is the use of ⟨u/v⟩ not only for earlier ⟨f⟩ internally (*heuenes*), which is a universal development in English, but for ⟨f⟩ initially also (*vader, uorlet, vri, uram*). During the eleventh century /f/

---

[1] In Scotland, printers followed a different tradition, replacing ⟨ʒ⟩ with its nearest equivalent in type, ⟨z⟩. Most Scottish words which retain this ⟨z⟩ now have a spelling-pronunciation in current English, ⟨z⟩ being pronounced /z/, but *Everyman's Pronouncing Dictionary* still records ⟨z⟩ for /j/ in *capercailzie, Dalziel, Menzies*.

[2] [ç] and [x] were allophones of /h/ in early Old English and were represented ⟨h⟩. But in many dialects of Middle English [h] had disappeared, and in view of the spelling ⟨ʒ⟩ it is possibly better to regard [ç] and [x] as allophones of /j/. Cf. also p. 27 footnote 1.

[3] In a few words the sounds [ç] and [x] were not lost but fell in with /f/, hence the anomalous ⟨gh⟩ for /f/ in *cough, laugh, tough*, etc.

[4] From British Museum MS Arundel 57.

initially was voiced in southern and western districts of England, and texts written in these areas indicate the voicing from the end of the twelfth century, spelling systems of other parts of the country retaining ⟨f⟩. Modern English orthography is based primarily on the variety of spelling used in the east midlands in the Middle English period (cf. p. 36) and hence most words which began with ⟨f⟩ in Old English do so today. There are a few exceptions, for example *vane* (OE *fana*), in which we have adopted a southern spelling, but since in all of them we have also adopted the southern pronunciation /v/, there is no disturbance of the sound-symbol relationship. Slightly anomalous, however, is our spelling (and pronunciation) of the feminine of *fox* as *vixen* /vɪksn/, where the influence of separate Middle English traditions has disturbed the relationship between etymologically and semantically related elements of our vocabulary.[1] The spelling *fixen* survived until the seventeenth century.

An important feature of passage vi is its complete orthographic consistency internally; the spelling *ine* 'in', for example, is maintained in all three instances. The final ⟨e⟩ here is unetymological, but it is a feature of Kentish orthography throughout Middle English.[2] It is extremely doubtful if this ⟨e⟩ were ever pronounced; it provides another illustration of the fact that the regional orthographies of Middle English were traditional writing systems rather than faithful phonemic ones. The preface to the book containing passage vi identifies the author as Dan Michel of Northgate, a monk of St Augustine's, Canterbury. The book is his own translation of a French text, written, as he states, in his own hand in the English of Kent, and completed in 1340. His manuscript is thus rather special—dated, localised, and an autograph. This explains the spelling consistency in the passage; at a time when there was no universal spelling, consistency could be maintained only if the author copied his own work (provided he himself had been properly trained) or if his work was copied by a scribe trained in the same regional orthography. The situation in

---

[1] The relationship is clearest in prehistoric times before the divergence of stem vowels (*fuhs-, *fuhsin-), but Old English spelling relates the two fairly well: *fox, fyxen*. The stem vowel development is comparable with that in Modern English *gold* and *gilden* or *gilt*.

[2] It is found in the 'Kentish' sermons recorded in the early thirteenth-century manuscript Laud 471 in the Bodleian Library, and in poems by William of Shoreham recorded in the fourteenth-century (cf. *The Religious Poems of William de Shoreham*, ed. T. Wright, Percy Society, London 1849.)

Middle English generally is that such texts as we have were written initially in one orth~graphy and copied by scribes familiar with another· Most texts have a long transmission history, and in the course of repeated copying, spellings which developed as regional forms over- lapped and became mere variants, available outside their area of origin. Some indication of the amount of orthographic inconsistency of the period can be seen in the following two versions of a doggerel verse Lord's Prayer:[1]

vii.	viii.
Fader oure þat is in heuen,	Owre fadur þat art in he**won**,
Blessid be þi name to neuen.[2]	Blessud be þi name to new**on**.
Come to vs þi kyngdome.	**Cum** to vs þi kyndome.
In heuen and erthe þi wille be done.	In he**won** and erthe þi **wyl** be done.
Oure ilk-day-bred graunt vs today,	Owre ilke dayus bred grawnt vs today,
And oure mysdedes forgyue vs ay.	And owre mysdedus for ʒyf vs ay.
Als we do hom[3] þat trespas us	As we do hom þat to vs trespas
Right so haue merci v‿on vs,	Ryght so haue mercy vpon vs,
And lede vs in no foundynge,	And lede vs into no fowndyng,
Bot shild vs fro al wicked þinge.	But schyld vs fro all wyccud þing.

Spelling differences between the passages are printed bold in viii to show the amount of variation which might be introduced into a text in the course of transmission (though it should be noted that, while the two copies are ultimately related, it cannot be assumed that one is a direct copy of the other). Both scribes alternate between ⟨i⟩ and ⟨y⟩ in stressed positions (vii has a preference for ⟨i⟩ except in *kyngdome* and *forgyue*, viii prefers ⟨y⟩ except in *ilke* and *þing*); both display a somewhat cavalier attitude to final ⟨e⟩ (less frequent in viii than in vii but added in *ilke*) and also to double consonants (*wille, wyl; al, all*); in closed unstressed syllables vii alternates ⟨i⟩ and ⟨e⟩ (*blessid, wicked*) while viii has ⟨u⟩ (*blessud, wiccud*); viii represents /v/ usually by ⟨w⟩ (*hewon*) but once by the ⟨u⟩ preferred by vii (*haue*). Not all of these variations are related to the use of different regional orthographies, but some are, and the potential for confusion caused by incomplete trans- mission from one system to another is obviously great.[4]

---

[1] Taken from the *Lay Folk's Mass Book*, British Museum MS Royal 17 B xvii and Gonville and Caius College, Cambridge, MS 84.162. The first is reproduced in plate 2.
[2] *neuen* 'name, repeat'.
[3] *hom* 'them'.
[4] Passage vii is north-east midlands of circa 1375, passage viii is west midlands of the mid-fifteenth century. Although the second passage was copied much later, the first is in general nearer to Modern English in spelling because the regional orthography

The existence of regional orthographies, and their confusion in the copying of texts resulted in a very lax attitude to spelling in most scribes. Few had been trained in the writing of English (for many it was secondary to the copying of French and Latin), and few bothered to maintain consistency. In a recently noted section of an early thirteenth-century copy of Laȝamon's *Brut* (a long poem on the early history of Britain which is notable for containing the first account in English of the Arthurian legend), the scribe made a purely mechanical error, and provided for us a revealing glimpse of the unreliability of the average copyist. By mistaking his place in his copy-text, he reproduced a section of the poem twice. The manuscript is shown in plate 3, where the duplicated passage can be seen roughly crossed through. There are a great many differences between the two versions, differences of syntax, of word-order, of inflection, and even of vocabulary.[1] On a purely orthographic level (leaving aside the complicated question of whether the differences provide material for the study of phonology) we have *heh, hæh; strengðe, strenðe; hælden, heolden; after, æfter; uaste, uæste; aȝein, aȝan; iwarð, iwræð*. If we wished to be generous to the scribe, we might suggest that the differences could have arisen because in one version he was being faithful to the spelling of his copy text, and in the other he was altering to his own convention. But the truth is more likely that he has no conception of a spelling standard, and used variant forms at will.

We have seen that the orthographic picture in Middle English is one of great variety. On the one hand there is the Canterbury monk Michel using a regional orthography consistently, an orthography that contains conventional spellings like *ine* which are some centuries old, and on the other hand there is the untrained or uncontrolled copyist of Laȝamon's *Brut*. On one side too we have the situation at Peterborough where the ability to use Old English spelling waned, while on another we have evidence of a scriptorium somewhere in the west midlands where knowledge of the Old English convention was not only retained but developed. The focal point of this continuity is the rich Anglo-Saxon diocese of Worcester, where early in the eleventh century Archbishop

in which it is written was important in the fifteenth-century creation of a national standard (cf. p. 36). Western features in passage viii are ⟨u⟩ to represent the unstressed vowel (⟨o⟩ after ⟨w⟩ in *hewon, newon*) and ⟨sch⟩ for /ʃ/ against the ⟨sh⟩ of passage vii (see p. 46).

[1] For a commentary see G. L. Brook, 'A piece of evidence for the study of Middle English spelling', *Neuphilologia Mitteilungen* 73 (1972), 25–8.

Wulfstan of York (died 1023), who held Worcester in plurality, founded an extensive English library. Throughout the century the Worcester scriptorium was very active in the copying of English writings, especially those of Abbot Ælfric, and long after the Norman Conquest, when English writing was on the decline everywhere else, Worcester continued to produce English books. Retention of the older tradition was aided at that time by the longevity of its bishop, another Wulfstan (subsequently canonised), the only Anglo-Saxon prelate to outlive the Conqueror and die in possession of his see. Even after St Wulfstan's death in 1095, the English tradition remained very much alive. Continued interest in the native language as a written medium in the twelfth century and later may be seen in a number of ways: in records of English books which were written (e.g. a life of St Wulfstan) even though they have not survived; in extant copies of earlier material made in twelfth-century Worcester (e.g. the large collection of homilies in Bodleian Library MS Bodley 343, which also contains a portrait of St Wulfstan); in the heavy glossing to which Worcester books of the earlier period were subjected throughout the later twelfth and the thirteenth century; and finally in the substantial corpus of new prose which appeared in the area around 1200. The body of new writing represents a revival of English prose, though the attempt to model the style of some of it, particularly the lives of three virgin saints, Juliana, Katharine and Margaret, on an alliterative prose which Ælfric had used for his lives of saints two centuries earlier underlines the continuity with the Old English tradition. There is also very close linguistic continuity, for the orthography of this prose is directly descended from the late West Saxon spelling system, with minor modifications characteristic of all Middle English texts (e.g. those already considered, ⟨ʒ⟩ alongside ⟨g⟩, ⟨u⟩ for /v/, etc., and other general developments of the thirteenth century such as ⟨ch⟩ for /tʃ/ considered in the next chapter).[1]

Two manuscripts are central to the study of this west midlands prose: Corpus Christi College, Cambridge, MS 402, containing a version of the text called *Ancrene Wisse* ('Anchoresses' knowledge'), and Bodleian Library MS Bodley 34, containing the saints' lives mentioned above, together with other religious pieces. The two manuscripts, written by different scribes and containing material very distinct in

[1] There are also a few innovations idiosyncratic to this system, e.g. ⟨h⟩ for /j/ internally, but these are no more numerous than one would expect to find in any system over a period of two centuries.

kind and quality, have a unique importance in early Middle English in that they employ an identical system of spelling and accidence. Their written di .lect is known to philologists as the AB language, 'A' for *Ancrene Wisse* and 'B' for Bodley 34. The spelling is so 'pure', i.e. unadulterated by copying scribes, that it seems inconceivable that it was not that employed by the authors. More than one author and at least two scribes using precisely the same orthography argues for a very strong tradition in existence in the west midlands early in the thirteenth century, and shows continued interest in the area in the careful training of scribes. It is interesting to note too that, despite very close linguistic links with West Saxon, certain features of the AB language, particularly the use of the grapheme ⟨ea⟩ for a group of words spelt with ⟨a⟩ in West Saxon, connect it with the Mercian literary language which antedates the West Saxon one of the later tenth century (cf. p. 6).[1] We may, then, be justified in postulating a continuous literary tradition in the west midlands extending over four centuries, from the middle of the ninth century until the thirteenth, though since no documentary evidence for the intervening centuries is available it is perhaps safer to think of AB as important only as a unique early Middle English development and as a significant link with late West Saxon.

As we have seen in connection with the collapse of the Old English standard, the crucial factor in the formation and maintenance of a uniform orthography is output; once output is reduced, the standard is lost. The flowering of religious prose in the west midlands at the turn of the twelfth century occurred just as the decline in the copying of Old English material was complete, or, if we allow for the life-span of the average scribe, just before the Old English tradition was forgotten.[2]

[1] In early Old English, ⟨ea⟩ represented a diphthong (though cf. p. 12, footnote 2) but monophthongisation took place towards the end of the period, and the resulting sound fell in with one already represented ⟨æ⟩. In AB, since the character ⟨æ⟩ was not used because of its similarity to ⟨e⟩ in the script, words with earlier ⟨ea⟩ and those with earlier ⟨æ⟩ were all represented ⟨ea⟩. A problem arises in a number of words which West Saxon spelt with ⟨a⟩ but which appear with ⟨ea⟩ in AB. These are anomalous since West Saxon ⟨a⟩ generally appears in AB as ⟨a⟩, and explanation for the use of ⟨ea⟩ may lie in the fact that they are all spelt with ⟨æ⟩ in ninth-century Mercian. A direct link (and perhaps one which could only occur through a continuous written tradition) is thus forged between the Mercian dialect of Old English and the AB language.

[2] The author of *Ancrene Wisse*, the most outstanding work of the thirteenth-century prose revival, deservedly popular in its own day and of considerable influence on religious writers of the following centuries, wrote what would appear to be an old-

For a short while in this remote area (remote from the court and the administration, at least), writings in English once again became numerous, and a uniform orthography heavily dependent upon the earlier standard was stabilised. Though the AB language in its pure form appears in only two extant manuscripts, individual spellings reminiscent of the dialect, particularly the distinctive ⟨ea⟩, can be traced in copies of a range of early Middle English religious literature, suggesting that its origin was in this literary language or that at some stage in its transmission it was copied in it. In other words, the west midlands regional variety became for a while a standard literary medium of English, but because it seems to have been a standard principally for religious material, and because it was not used very widely outside its area of origin, its time of glory was comparatively short.

More or less contemporary with the scribes of the AB language, but working in the east rather than the west midlands, an Augustinian canon called Orm produced a manuscript which is also of significance in the history of spelling. This curious document is one of the most remarkable survivals from the Middle Ages. Full of corrections, alterations, additions in the margins and on inserted part leaves, it is certainly Orm's own copy, and with the translation of Michel of Canterbury it provides an opportunity to study a medieval author's autograph manuscript. The work is a verse homiliary of 10,000 long lines written in a consistent orthography of Orm's invention. The spelling is a carefully considered one, improvements in the system being incorporated in the course of the manuscript (with the earlier portion altered accordingly), and many mistakes in the transcription being corrected. The idea behind the revised spelling would appear to be a desire to improve the delivery of the preachers who used the sermons by creating a phonemic spelling. There is no evidence of the book, which its author called the *Ormulum*, having enjoyed any success in its own day, but it has become very popular recently among scholars interested in phonology. Two of the most notable features of the system, illustrated in plate 4, are the doubling of consonants to show that a preceding vowel in a closed syllable is short, and the creation of three

fashioned AB (i.e. he has more features reminiscent of late Old English than are to be found in Bodley 34 and Corpus Christi 402), and was perhaps taught in his youth to spell according to the West Saxon tradition (cf. his use of ⟨c⟩ for /tʃ/ and ⟨sc⟩ for /ʃ/ rather than the thirteenth-century developments ⟨ch⟩ and ⟨sch⟩). Cf. E. J. Dobson, 'The Affiliations of the manuscripts of *Ancrene Wisse*', *English and Medieval Studies presented to J. R. R. Tolkien*, edited by Norman Davis and C. L. Wrenn, London 1962.

(*Plate 4*) The *Ormulum*, Bodleian Library MS Junius I (circa 1200) upper part of fol. 3r. Note the superscript letters, some of which represent the author's revisions.

Transliteration of the first twelve lines of the manuscript:

Nu broþerr wallt. broþerr min.
Afft þe flæshess kide. 7 broþerr
min i cristenndom. þurrh ful-
luhht. 7 þurrh trowᵂþe. 7 broþerr min i ᵹodess hus. ᵹ̃t o þe þri-
de wise. Þurrh þatt witt hafenn
tákenᵘ ba. An reᵹ̃hell boc to fóllᵹhenn. Vnn-
derr kanunnkess had. 7 lif. Swa summ sannt
Awwstin setteˢ Icc hafe don swa summ þu badd. 7
forþedd te þin wille. ¶ Icc hafe wenᵘd inᵖtill enn-
glissh. ᵹoddspelless hallᵹhe lâreˢ Afft þ littleˢ
witt tattᵉ* me. Min drihhtin hafeþᵖ lenedd.

Translation:

Now brother Walter, my brother
by way of nature, and my brother
in Christianity, through
baptism and through faith, and
even in the third way my brother in
God's house, in that we have
both undertaken to follow the Rule
for the state and life of a canon that St
Augustine laid down. I have done as you asked, and
carried out your wishes. I have turned into
English the holy teaching of the Gospel by means of
the little wit that my Lord has granted me.

* altered from patt

Plate 4

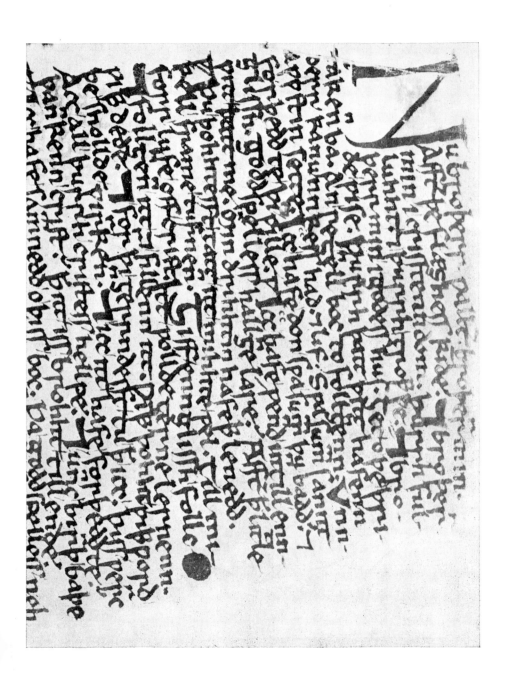

Plate 5

The first Wycliffite version of the Bible, British Museum MS Royal 1 B vi (circa 1400) fol. 18r. Passage ix (p. 31) begins on line 9, column 1.

graphemes to replace Old English ⟨ȝ⟩: the Old English symbol retained for the sound /j/, a clever blend of the Old English symbol with the carolingian ⟨g⟩ for /g/, and the carolingian ⟨g⟩ itself used in an occasional French loanword with /dʒ/ (and ⟨gg⟩ for the native phoneme /dʒ/ which occurred only medially or finally). Orm anticipated some of the techniques of phonemic spelling reformers by many centuries, for example in consistency of spelling and in an attempted correlation of phoneme and grapheme. The lack of contemporary documents makes it difficult to be sure how far he was innovating in usages which have later become established in standard spelling, but as his manuscript is the first to record ⟨wh⟩ for earlier ⟨hw⟩ and ⟨sh⟩ for earlier ⟨sc⟩ (cf. pp. 46–7), we might be justified in crediting him at least with happy anticipation of later developments if not in actually influencing them.

For a uniform orthography of wider distribution we have to wait until the fourteenth century, when, as with the AB language, the activities of religious writers were again responsible for the appearance of a standard literary form. This time it was the creation of John Wyclif (1320–84) and his Lollard followers, whose considerable English writings of the later fourteenth century, in particular the Bible translations which survive in some 170 manuscripts, were spread throughout the country in copies utilising an orthography based on that native to the central midlands, an area stretching roughly from Oxford to Cambridge and as far north as Leicester. Early in the fifteenth century, scribes in many parts of England were using the orthography made fashionable by the Lollards not only for Wycliffite texts but for a great deal of material of the more orthodox religious writers of the fourteenth century, those writing in the literary tradition of *Ancrene Wisse* such as Richard Rolle and Walter Hilton. Even non-religious writings are occasionally to be found with the same spelling system, and, had the Lollards retained their popularity throughout the fifteenth century, it might have become the standard that we use today. But it seems to have fallen from grace with its principal purveyors. The following sample of it is taken from the earlier Bible translation of the 1380s:[1]

ix.
Oure fadir, þat art in heuenys, halewid be þi name. Þi kyngdom come to. Be þi

[1] Taken from British Museum MS Royal 1 B vi, which is reproduced in plate 5. The many abbreviations of the manuscript are here expanded silently.

4

wille don as in heuene and in erþe. ʒiue to us þis day oure breed ouer oþer substaunse. And forʒiue to us oure dettes, as and we forʒiuen to oure dettouris. And leede us not into temptacioun, but delyuere us from yuel.

Clearly this is much nearer Modern English than anything illustrated in this chapter so far, but in part this is because the vocabulary and syntax are closer to our own. The spelling is still very different. Particularly noteworthy is the absence of the grapheme ⟨ea⟩ so frequently used in Modern English: cf. *heuene, erþe, breed, leede*.[1] The spelling of 'father' with medial ⟨d⟩, which has been seen in all of the passages so far cited, remained until the sixteenth century when intervocalic /d/ became /ð/.[2] A number of spellings indicate dialectal differences between the basis of this writing system and that which gave rise to Modern English orthography, e.g. *ʒiue, forʒiuen, yuel*, and the unstressed syllables of *fadir, heuenys, halewid, dettouris*. The form *yuel* and its modern counterpart *evil* have different initial vowels because of separate Middle English traditions in the development of Old English ⟨y⟩ (cf. pp. 19–22). The verbs *ʒiue, forʒiuen* and their corresponding Modern English form (–)*give* show differences which developed in Middle English dialects as a result of the influence of the language spoken by the Danish and Norwegian vikings who settled in eastern and northern parts of England from the ninth to the eleventh centuries. Just as the use, or at least the comprehension, of French by a large proportion of the population of England in the twelfth and early thirteenth centuries caused the adoption into English of a great many French words (cf. chapter 3), so the use of two languages in the areas of Norse settlement at a slightly earlier period created considerable overlapping of elements from both languages in the English dialects of those areas. Norse influence was not confined to loanwords, however. Like English, Norse is a Germanic language, and though sound-

[1] The source of ⟨ea⟩ in the modern forms of these words is discussed below, p. 48. ⟨ea⟩ in them is not an indication of influence of the AB language on modern spelling, though the popularity of ⟨ea⟩ in the modern convention is perhaps in part the result of the widespread use of the grapheme in AB. (The AB spellings of the four words involved retain the Old English vowel graphemes in *heouen, eorðe, bread* (OE *heofon, eorðe, bread*) and supply ⟨ea⟩ for ⟨æ⟩ in *leaden*, OE *lædan*.)

[2] This sound-change explains a number of words alternating in spelling between ⟨-d-⟩ and ⟨-th-⟩ in Tudor English. Most have now established themselves with ⟨th⟩ and /ð/ (e.g. *father, further, gather, hither, mother, together, weather*), but two, *burden* and *murder*, retain ⟨d⟩ and /d/ (probably because of French influence). *Burthen* and *murther* will be familiar to readers of Shakespeare and the King James Bible in old-spelling editions.

changes had caused differences to develop between the two, a large stock of basic words were sufficiently close in form for the development of some English words to be influenced by their Norse counterparts. Thus Modern English *give* has the stem vowel of the Old English (late West Saxon) verb ȝyfan (pronounced /jivǝn/), but the initial consonant is from Norse *gefa* (pronounced /geva/). The Wycliffite dialect preserves the native form intact. Finally the use of ⟨i/y⟩ in unstressed syllables is an east and central midlands feature commented upon on p. 25.

If the ambulatory kings of the Middle Ages had settled in Hereford or Worcester, or even in Gloucester where they frequently held court, the antecedent of the modern spelling system would probably have been not unlike the AB language. If Oxford, another favourite royal centre, had been chosen, then modern spelling might have developed from the Wycliffite literary standard. But the court settled in London, and as the capital grew in size, in administrative importance, and in wealth, the language spoken and, more particularly, written there increased in authority. Standard written English used today as a world language, and the spelling convention which broadly is part of that standard, were established in London in the fifteenth century, and it is to the dialect of the London area that we must now turn.

Politically London was the capital of the early Anglo-Saxon kingdom of Essex. Its population and prosperity grew rapidly in the last century before the Norman Conquest, when it was particularly benefited by England's expanding economy and trade with northern Europe, and its prominence was assured by its selection as the seat of his government by Edward the Confessor (1042–66). Dialectally, London at first formed part of the Essex area, if we trust to the scanty records of the early Middle English period, but its importance and wealth attracted a constant flow of immigrants from many areas of the country. It is hardly surprising to find that the city, with its shifting and heterogeneous population had no strong orthographic tradition as more static communities such as those of Canterbury or the west midlands did. Nor is it surprising that a standard like that of the Wycliffites did not appear. Wycliffite spelling spread throughout the country because its users sought to identify themselves by the adoption of a linguistic medium associated with their particular religious movement, but no such community of interest existed to influence writers in London. Furthermore, not only were there great differences of dialect and interest amongst London writers at the end of the fourteenth century but range of technical skill was also very considerable. Surviving examples of pre-Conquest writing are in the main the products of professional scribes taught to spell in the rigorously controlled conditions of monastic scriptoria, but written material from fourteenth-century London is of a much more varied nature. As society became more complex in the later Middle Ages, the need of each household of any importance for a member who could read and write became proportionately greater. In many wealthy houses the chaplain still fulfilled the function, but by the end of the fourteenth century there were numerous prosperous merchants employing secular clerks whose whole time was occupied with secretarial work. The founding of the universities and the increased wealth of the merchant classes led to education being spread more liberally through society, and the consequent demand for books, which was to lead in a short while to the invention of printing, had the more immediate effect of divorcing book-production from the monasteries and establishing the secular trade of scrivener. The growing complexity of mercantile society, the increased literacy of the lay population, and the introduction of paper, which put permanent writing within the reach of a larger proportion of the population than was possible with expensive parchment, all made conditions very different from those of the Old English period. Consequently, extant writings from fourteenth-century London run right through the scale of professionalism from the products of the scriveners and clerks to those of men who had had little schooling. Orthographic training, à necessary condition of the establishment of a literary standard, was frequently lacking.

When Chaucer died in 1400, only the Wycliffite dialect had any widespread authority as a literary standard in England. London writings, including those of professional writers, show a considerable mixture of forms from southern dialects, from the central midlands standard of the Lollards, and also from more northern and eastern areas, the result of the absorption of population from the rich and populous areas of Norfolk, Lincolnshire and Yorkshire. Not until a body of professional scribes with a close common bond appeared in London was a uniform orthography established there, and such a body was not supplied until the scribes of the royal chancery adopted English as their usual written medium.

In France, the history of spelling stabilisation is closely bound to the development of legal language, but in England legal documents, headed by those stemming from the chancery, were for a long period in Latin, or, if the vernacular were used at all, in French. If we look back to the Old English period, we find that English was the established language of administrative documents in the last century and a half of Anglo-Saxon rule, and though insufficient authentic products of the pre-Conquest royal secretariat survive to show how far central direction was given to spelling by the king's writing-house, it is likely that the orthography used by royal clerks, distributed as it was throughout the country by means of government writs, played some part in promoting a uniform spelling tradition everywhere in the kingdom in the early eleventh century. The authority given to the West Saxon orthography in this way was lost with the change of language in chancery documents which took place about 1070. The discarding of English was not a policy step on the Conqueror's part aimed at debasing the native language but one necessitated by a change in the population of the chancery. Clerks of the king's secretariat were well placed for receiving rewards in the shape of high office even in pre-Conquest times, many an Anglo-Saxon bishop having had a period in the king's clerical service before gaining episcopal rank. It is unlikely that native clerks would remain in such influential positions for long after William's victory, and they were replaced by men with a comparatively slight knowledge of English who naturally assumed the bureaucratic language of Normandy, Latin.

However, early in the fifteenth century the chancery once more began to issue documents in English, considerable numbers appearing from about 1430. This gave professional scribes outside the chancery the lead they had been waiting for. Scriveners in large towns throughout the country began to imitate the spellings of chancery scribes, and since scriveners, like other tradesmen, took on apprentices who were taught to follow their master's example in all the practices of their trade, not least spelling, there grew up the forerunner of the house-style still used in publishing today whereby each commercial concern has a style-sheet which lays down a pattern for the products of the house. The incentives towards consistency which influenced the scriveners (apprenticeship training, the frequency with which individual words occurred, and the need to produce copy which would not displease a customer by irregular or perhaps dialectal forms) did not apply to the non-professional writer, but the desire to imitate the products of the capital and to avoid the censure of provinciality did nevertheless lead during the course of the fifteenth century to the abandoning of regional orthographies in favour of that of chancery English.

Much has been said of the influence of chancery spelling without any consideration of its background. The Anglo-Saxon kings' capital was Winchester, and the Old English chancery spelling was thus established in the heart of Wessex. Edward the Confessor began the movement towards London by founding an abbey some miles to the west of the city on a site subsequently called Westminster, and by the reign of Henry II (1154–89) the whole of the chancery had been moved to the royal abbey. In the fourteenth century, as clerical influence in the chancery declined, a further move to the city itself (Chancery Lane) took place, though the earlier association of the administration with Westminster remains to the present day. The dialect of English adopted by chancery scribes when they abandoned French and Latin in the fifteenth century was thus that in use in the Greater London area. The spelling system is distinct from that used by Chaucer in the same city half a century earlier, for London orthography in Chaucer's day was considerably confused and still subject to the influence of immigrants. Since much of the immigration in the early years of the fifteenth century was from the central and east midlands, the dialects of these areas played an important part in the formation of chancery spelling. In fact the orthography has much in common with the central midlands standard adopted by Wyclif, but is nevertheless distinct because it stabilised half a century later and because it was based on the speech of a linguistically less homogeneous group. The midlands element is a basic one however, and it is not too much of a simplification to call Modern Standard English a development of the east midlands variety of Middle English, though it is important to remember too that the south, particularly the south-east, was also influential.

Further consideration of the development of chancery spelling must include an examination of the influence on it of Anglo-Norman, the language of many chancery documents of the period immediately preceding the adoption of English, and this will be more appropriate in the next chapter. The dialects cannot be left, however, before mention is made of one system which is first recorded only comparatively late in the Middle English period, but which, because of political separation, continued to be used long after the others had disappeared. The heyday of Scottish English was in the fifteenth and sixteenth centuries, and though northern writers tended to use Standard English after the union of the Scottish and English crowns in 1603, Scots remains the one British dialect which may be represented today by a consistent (and traditional) orthography. An illustration of its early form is the following text, copied circa 1520:[1]

x.
Our fader, that art in heuenis, hallewit be thi name. Thi kingdom cum to. Thi wil be done in erde as in heuen. Gefe to vs this day our breid ouer vthir substance. And forgif to vs our dettis, as we forgef to our dettouris. And leid vs nocht into temptatioun, bot deliuer vs fra euile.

The translation is based on the Lollard Bible, and some southern influence is inevitable; the spelling of *euile*, for example, by this date was universal. But there are many characteristic Scottish forms, for example *cum, erde, bot* are the usual forms of *come, earth, but* throughout Middle Scots, and ⟨ch⟩ in *nocht* represents a velar fricative which, because it is no longer heard in southern English, is one of the more widely recognised phonemes of northern dialect.[2] Lowland Scotland, like northern England, was an area of Norse settlement (cf. pp. 4 and 32), and *gefe, forgef* and *fra* are Scandinavian forms etymologically. Two uses of ⟨i⟩ are notable: one is its frequent appearance in unstressed syllables (*heuenis, hallewit, vthir, dettis, dettouris*), a feature of north-eastern spelling which has been noted already (pp. 25 and 33); the other is the use of ⟨i⟩ as a diacritic of vowel length in *breid* and *leid*.[3] Diacritic ⟨i⟩ is one of the more familiar conventions of Scots spelling; cf. *haim, mair, guid, buik* for *home, more, good, book*.[4] The convention appears in Standard English in words that have been drawn from Scots dialect, e.g. *raid*, the northern cognate of *road* (OE *rad*) which was carried south by Sir Walter Scott.

This chapter has concentrated on illustrating the variety of spelling in Middle English caused by the use of regional orthographies, but variety in the period was also the result of scribes' familiarity with the conventions of languages other than English, and it is to this subject that the next chapter moves.

[1] Taken from *The New Testament in Scots*, ed. Thomas Graves Law, The Scottish Text Society, Edinburgh and London 1901.
[2] The word in Old English is *noht*, surviving in Standard English as *nought* (stressed) and *not* (unstressed); cf. p. 23. On ⟨ch⟩ in early northern English, cf. p. 11.
[3] The vowel of *breid*, Mod. E *bread*, has since been shortened in RP but remains long in some northern dialects.
[4] Again what were once long vowels in all dialects in these words have become short vowels or diphthongs in RP.

Chapter 3   The French invasion

It was once fashionable to suggest that the foundations of modern British social institutions were laid by the Norman conquerors and that little or no continuity could be traced between Anglo-Saxon civilisation and that of the present day. But more recently historians have stressed that 1066 marked principally a change of dynasty in England, and that Anglo-Norman society was not so very different from that of Anglo-Saxon times. Many of the greatest administrative achievements of the Normans rest on the successful development of native institutions, and it would have been strange therefore if the vast Anglo-Saxon book-producing machine which had added so substantially to England's material and spiritual wealth in the first half of the eleventh century had been allowed to founder. It is true that during the second half of the century the output of books in English gradually dwindled, but this was only as the monastic scriptoria adjusted themselves to the demands of their new rulers. By the twelfth century reorganisation was complete, and by means of an enormous programme of translation the religious thought of the age was made available to French readers as it had been made available to English readers a hundred and fifty years earlier. French became the written vernacular of England.

The result is that many of the earliest and best versions of Old French literary works are in Anglo-Norman, the name given to the dialect of French used in England. Records of French do not become at all numerous until the twelfth century, and large numbers of the surviving manuscripts are products of English scriptoria. But the importance of Anglo-Norman was short-lived. By the middle of the twelfth century, writers in France had established a reasonably accurate phonemic spelling, and from then on continental French orthography remained relatively stable. Its concrete spelling system was a source of difficulty for Anglo-Norman scribes, however, for in England a different orthographic tradition existed, and though this had been created for the recording of English, knowledge of it was sufficiently widespread to cause confusion. Furthermore Anglo-Norman as a dialect became increasingly divorced from the French of France. The English crown's loss of Normandy in 1204 marked the beginning of the physical separation of the Anglo-Norman aristocracy from their lands in France, and the 'national' wars of the Edwards, the First's against Scotland and the Third's against France, tended to underline the insular interests of French speakers in England. Though French remained a prestige language for a long time, many people being reluctant to see the linguistic indicator of rank lost, ultimately the community could not support two vernaculars. Long before the end of the fourteenth century French was artificially maintained in schools as pupils were forced to construe their Latin into French rather than English, while students at Oxford were forbidden to speak in English. Parliament was not conducted officially in English until 1362, and the law continued to rely heavily on French until much later, lawyers of the sixteenth century still averring that English was too insensitive an instrument for so precise a machine as the legal one. (To the present day legal register contains a larger element of French phraseology than the standard language.) But the decline of French in England is made clear by the appearance during the thirteenth century of manuals for its correct use. Before 1300 for the majority of Englishmen, French was an acquired language, and in the course of the fourteenth century this became true of all ranks of society, even as high as the court. Anglo-Norman, except as a legal language, was dead.

In part the decline of Anglo-Norman was due to increasing realisation that it had become different from continental French. By the fourteenth century French was important internationally as the language of diplomacy and to some extent of religion, while French literature and culture were everywhere admired. Travel in Europe, a period in the University of Paris, and knowledge of the work of the most outstanding teachers and writers of the day were all facilitated by an understanding of French, but what was required was the ability to use not the provincial and barbarous Anglo-Norman but the cultured and sophisticated Parisian French. Hence the French linguistic invasion of England in the high Middle Ages was a prolonged compaign. It began with French used as a separate written and spoken language in England alongside English. Then, as Anglo-Norman declined, speakers ceased to be bilingual to the extent of using French grammar, but in changing over to English carried a large part of the vocabulary of French with them. Later again, Parisian French became a prestige language, while Anglo-Norman continued to influence the legal language which, because it was familiar to chancery scribes, was important in the development of Standard English. All fronts of the invasion may be shown to be of significance for the history of spelling.

We may begin by examining some of the effects of bilingualism in England. The most obvious is that a large proportion of present-day English vocabulary is derived from French. A dictionary count might put it as high as forty per cent, though the number of French borrowings in the average English sentence is much smaller because most of the basic and commonest words are English (i.e. inherited from Old English). Most of the French loanwords appear in English for the first time in the Middle English period, a great many of them no doubt in the twelfth and early thirteenth centuries when the two languages were used and understood by large numbers of people in all but the very lowest social orders. Because an extensive range of vocabulary was borrowed in a comparatively short period at a time when a large proportion of native English speakers had some familiarity with French, the phonemic pattern of English was altered marginally. Normally loanwords adopted from one language to another are forced to accord with the sound patterns of the recipient language. A simple example is the modern borrowing *courgette*, which in English is pronounced /kɔ:ʒet/ as against French /kuʀʒet/.[1] But borrowings during the period of bilingualism retained the pronunciation of the parent language, for example in *choice* we have a diphthong /ɔɪ/ which occurs in English only in loanwords. The spelling of such words follows the French usage of the day, though ⟨y⟩ now replaces ⟨i⟩ finally or before another vowel (*coy, royal*). Not all of the French phonemic structure could be assimilated, of course, and parts of it noticeably foreign to English were excluded. An example may be seen in the French nasalised vowels, which tended to be denasalised in English, cf. French *gentil* /ʒɑ̃ti/ and English *gentle* /dʒentl/. But in many words with Old French /ã/, Middle English spellings with ⟨an⟩ or ⟨aun⟩

---

[1] More extreme cases of alterations of this sort come under the heading of popular or folk etymology, e.g. Fr. *mousseron*, which was borrowed into English in the fifteenth century when French had ceased to be widely used in England, has become *mushroom*, each syllable being associated with a recognisable English morpheme.

(*chaunce, daunce, daunger, desperaunce*, etc)[1] show some attempt at representing the nasal vowel. In a few words the ⟨au⟩ spelling remains in Modern English, e.g. *haunt, jaundice, vaunt* (with a pronunciation /ɔ:/).[2]

A special problem introduced by the use of French pronunciation and French spelling affects borrowings which begin with ⟨h⟩. The aspirate was lost in Latin pronunciation soon after the classical period, and French has consequently never had an aspirate in that part of its vocabulary which is derived from Latin (i.e. the greater part). However, the influence of Classical Latin spelling was so strong on scribes during the Old French period that ⟨h⟩ frequently appears in the written language where no /h/ was heard in speech, and a great many Romance words with unpronounced ⟨h⟩ were borrowed into Middle English. They fall into three groups: (*a*) a small number in which ⟨h⟩ has been lost, e.g. *able, ability, arbour* (compare the first two with Modern French *habile, habilité*; the third is from Latin *herbarium*);[3] (*b*) rather more in which spelling preserves ⟨h⟩ but pronunciation is without /h/, e.g. *heir, honour, honest, hour;* (*c*) the majority, in which spelling-pronunciation (i.e. the acceptance of the spelling as indicative of historically correct pronunciation) has reintroduced /h/, e.g. *horrible, hospital, host.*[4]

---

[1] Cf. *substaunse* in the Wycliffite Lord's Prayer, passage ix (p. 32).

[2] An exception is *aunt* /ɑ:nt/, where ⟨au⟩ has been retained though the vowel is that of *chance, dance*, etc; here ⟨au⟩ may result from a conscious attempt to avoid confusion with *ant*. A parallel case of ⟨au⟩ corresponding to /ɑ:/ is provided by *staunch*, variant of *stanch*, but this is due to the falling together of the verb *stanch* with the adjective *staunch*.

[3] Also *ostler*, with a variant spelling *hostler*.

[4] In many ways spelling-pronunciation has been of importance in narrowing the gap between the written and spoken languages, particularly during the last few centuries as literacy has spread (cf. p. 55 below). It frequently appears in cases in which historical consonant groups have been simplified in speech while the spelling survives unchanged and supports the restoration of the lost consonant (e.g. /t/ is frequently heard now in *often, Christmas, postman*), but it is perhaps nowhere so potent as in the retention of the English aspirate. So strong is the influence of spelling here that no Old English word with initial ⟨h⟩ (with the possible exception of *it*, OE *hit*) has lost its aspirate in the course of the history of English, despite the fact that all regional dialects of southern English lost the phoneme /h/ during the Middle English period. (The confusion over /h/ in speakers of regional dialects today is the result of this loss.) Care over the matching of /h/ to ⟨h⟩ has likewise led literate speakers to introduce an aspirate in most French loanwords with ⟨h⟩, and it is interesting to see how the process has extended over many centuries. Orthoepists of the sixteenth and seventeenth centuries (cf. p. 93) indicate no /h/ in such words as *habit, harmonious* and *heritage*; Dr Johnson in the eighteenth century records no aspirate in *herb, humble* and *humour* (and references to pronunciation of these without the aspirate are common throughout nineteenth-century literature); and even today the use of the article *an* rather than *a*

The fact that most of the French loanwords discussed in the last two paragraphs have retained in English their French spelling is an indication of the extent to which French conventions penetrated English. The absorption of loanwords into a language does not inevitably carry with it the corollary of disturbance of the orthography. Latin, for example, provided the earliest phases of English with a large lexical element, and though it is obvious that those words borrowed in the pre-literate period will owe nothing in their modern spelling to the forms from which they ultimately derive (cf. Mod. E *cheese* and Classical Latin *caseus*), even the learned loanwords of the late Old English period, borrowed into the *written* language at a time when scribes often show consciousness of Latin forms, incorporate changes which make them accord with the patterns of the established spelling system. For example, Latin *diaconus* appears in Old English as *deacon* because the sequence ⟨ia⟩ never occurred in the native language; similarly Latin *phoenix* was transcribed *fenix* in Old English for the benefit of a reader not familiar with Latin orthography. As long as the West Saxon scribal tradition remained undisturbed, such anglicisations continued. Immediately after the Conquest, French borrowings were similarly treated: in an *Anglo-Saxon Chronicle* entry for 1070 the French word 'service' appears in the form *serfise*, with medial ⟨f⟩ for /v/.[1] But by the end of the twelfth century, cultured Englishmen were not only bilingual but also biliterate; many words of the vast influx from French into English were already familiar to Englishmen not only in French as a spoken language but in French writings too. What was required of such words in English writings was not an anglicised spelling (which might serve to remind readers of the pronunciation) but the spelling by which they were traditionally represented in French, however ill that accorded with English conventions. Consequently in the AB language, which continued the stable orthographic traditions of Old

in literary English before such words as *hotel* and *historical* suggests that they were pronounced without /h/ even more recently.

The history of the pronoun *it* is worthy of special note. Though it is usually spelt *hit* by Old English scribes, it is possible that ⟨h⟩ is unhistoric, being introduced to make the word parallel the oblique forms *his* (genitive) and *him* (dative). All three in the unstressed positions in which they normally appeared in speech would be without /h/. Cf. E. Prokosch, *A Comparative Germanic Grammar*, Philadelphia 1939, p. 275.

[1] Final ⟨e⟩ here is an accusative inflection; the nominative would presumably be *serfis*. It should be noted that only the change from ⟨u/v⟩ to ⟨f⟩ is relevant here. The usual French form of the period was *servise*, the spelling *service* being fixed later in both languages.

English (cf. pp. 27–9), French borrowings appear with French spelling. For example, the loanword *grace*, which in French traditionally had ⟨c⟩ though the sound represented had become identical with that normally represented ⟨s⟩, appears in its French form. In AB, such French conventions as ⟨c⟩ for /s/ are confined to those French words in which they were traditional, and English words retain in their turn their own traditional representation. But not all writers of English in the thirteenth century had the benefit of the strict orthographic training of AB scribes. In most areas, writing in the native language had diminished so considerably that traditional spelling had become disturbed, so much so that phonemic spellings based on the conventions of French orthography often appeared. In some native words these have survived; examples of ⟨c⟩ for /s/ occur in *cinder* and *ice* (OE *sinder, is*) and there are even two instances of disturbance within a paradigm: *mice* and *lice* as the plurals of *mouse* and *louse* (OE *mus, mys; lus, lys*).[1]

Most manuscripts of the thirteenth century which contain English material also have items by the same scribe in French, and orthographic confusion between the two languages is not surprising. But there is a further problem affecting this period which should also be noted. Latin provided a third set of spelling conventions to cause additional confusion in a situation already very fluid. Throughout the Old English period scribes were trained to copy Latin as well as English material, but little disturbance of the orthography resulted because the two languages were kept very separate, even to the extent of the use of two quite distinct scripts (cf. p. 22).[2] French scribes, on the other hand, were considerably influenced by Latin conventions (partly no doubt because of the close relationship of the two languages) and some of this influence rubbed off on their Middle English counterparts. In particular, the Late Latin practice of using ⟨o⟩ for earlier ⟨u⟩ caused

[1] The fixing of ⟨c⟩ for /s/ in English was aided by the fact that in many words with the final sequence ⟨se⟩ the consonant sound represented was /z/, e.g. *lose, surprise, wise*. Use of ⟨ce⟩ in the final position thus clarified the representation of final /s/: *ace, pence, since*. The device was particularly useful in noun/verb pairs where the spelling difference reflects one in pronunciation: *advice, advise; device, devise*, and in the seventeenth century it was extended by spelling book compilers to similar pairs which involve no sound change: *licence, license; practice, practise*. American usage has preferred ⟨se⟩ in all such cases since Noah Webster.

[2] Some influence is nonetheless discernible, e.g. the falling together of ⟨i⟩ and ⟨y⟩ in one grapheme is in part the result of imitation of Latin practice. Later, as the West Saxon tradition was lost and before French orthography was stabilised, Latin conventions were frequently used alongside English ones; cf. p. 17 and footnote.

some falling together of the two graphemes in French and later in English. Thus ⟨o⟩ replaced ⟨u⟩ in a large number of words with a short vowel, most of which now have RP /ʌ/ (e.g. *come, some, Somerset, monk, son, tongue, wonder, honey, worry, above, dove, love*), though some preserve the close vowel, RP /ʊ/ (*wolf, woman*). The use of ⟨o⟩ was valuable in distinguishing the vowel from a neighbouring consonant, particularly ⟨v⟩ (identical with ⟨u⟩ at this time, cf. p. 81) and ⟨w⟩ (written ⟨uu⟩, as the name of the letter suggests). The fact that the convention survives also in the neighbourhood of ⟨n⟩ and ⟨m⟩ has led many commentators to suggest that ⟨o⟩ was preferred to ⟨u⟩ to make reading easier, since the characters ⟨u n m⟩ all consisted in bookhand[1] of a series of minims (or straight down-strokes), the series in ⟨un ini iui uu iw im⟩ etc. being in danger of being misdivided and of causing confusion. It is an argument that is hard to accept for the native language, since it is unlikely that English readers of the Middle Ages read letter by letter any more than modern readers do, but it is possible that such an explanation may hold for Latin, where ⟨o⟩ for ⟨u⟩ first appeared. In English, indeed, ⟨o⟩ for ⟨u⟩ also appeared occasionally in words in which there was no danger of minim confusion (cf. Mod. E *borough, thorough*), and the convention may have been established in part because of an English sound change whereby /ɒ/ became /u/ (now RP /ʌ/), e.g. *among, money*.[2]

Some foreign conventions such as ⟨c⟩ for /s/ and ⟨o⟩ for /ʌ/ have come into English as it were accidentally, for they are the result of scribes' confusion between English, French and Latin spelling, and, since confusion rarely produces order, they provide anomalies in the contemporary spelling system, existing alongside alternative representations of /s/ and /ʌ/. But confusion in such marginal areas should not disguise the fact that knowledge of foreign conventions also brought English scribes some benefits, in that it enabled them to effect improvement in the native system where this was needed. Such a one is the use of ⟨ch⟩ for the phoneme /tʃ/. The grapheme was taken from Anglo-

---

[1] Two scripts were used in later medieval writings, a formal one for books (bookhand), with angular characters and heavy vertical minims (for example, plate 5), and a cursive script (secretary-hand) for documents and less permanent writings.

[2] Though ⟨o⟩ for /ʌ/ is a widespread convention in current English spelling, it should perhaps be observed that a great many words survive with ⟨u⟩, e.g. *hunt, under, humble, thumb*. The use of ⟨o⟩/⟨u⟩ to avoid homophones becoming homographs as well is also worth noting: *some, sum; son, sun; ton, tun.* Similarly ⟨u⟩ is perhaps preserved in *nut* to avoid confusion with *not.*

Norman about 1200 and appears consistently in thirteenth-century texts, including those of the AB language. The spread of ⟨ch⟩ is so complete and so fast that it must have fulfilled a need felt everywhere for unambiguous expression of the sound.[1] A problem had arisen in the Old English period when the two allophones of /k/, palatal before front vowels and velar before back ones, were disturbed by a vowel mutation which introduced front vowels after the velar allophone. As the earlier palatal had by this time become an affricate, the modern minimum pair *kin* and *chin* /kɪn:tʃɪn/ was created: in other words, sounds which were earlier positional variants became contrastive, allophones became phonemes. But Old English orthography continued to represent the two sounds by ⟨c⟩ (i.e. both of these words in late Old English were spelt *cinn* or *cynn*). Although ⟨c⟩ could still unambiguously represent /k/ before back vowels and consonants (as it still does in *cat, cot, cut, climb, crumb*), there was no agreed way of distinguishing the sounds graphically before front vowels. The use of ⟨k⟩ for the plosive appeared sporadically from the ninth century but it was not until the thirteenth that it was fully established in words like *king* and *keen*, by which time ⟨ch⟩ had been adopted for the affricate.[2]

The replacement of Old English ⟨c⟩ for /tʃ/ by ⟨ch⟩ carried with it

[1] Incorrect use of ⟨ch⟩, either its appearance for other sounds or its miswriting as ⟨hc⟩, is rare; the occasional use of ⟨c⟩, the Old English grapheme corresponding to /tʃ/, after the introduction of ⟨ch⟩ is probably an archaism.

[2] Thus Modern English spelling is doubly careful to represent /k/ and /tʃ/ separately, and were it not for later foreign influence, present-day use of two symbols ⟨c⟩ and ⟨k⟩ for the former, and the digraph ⟨ch⟩ for the latter would be acceptably unambiguous if unnecessarily cumbersome. But English is a language which has borrowed words from many languages, and from the same language at different periods; consequently an overlaying of many orthographic conventions has resulted, particularly when the borrowings are of a literary nature and have established themselves in the written language in the form obtaining in the parent language. Thus, to take examples of the sounds and spellings under discussion, Modern French borrowings have given us such words as *chauffeur* and *machine*, in which ⟨ch⟩ represents /ʃ/ (the Modern French development of earlier /tʃ/), while ⟨ch⟩ for /k/ appears in Latin borrowings like *chorus* and *archive*. ⟨c⟩ is no longer unambiguous not only because of the French-derived use of it for /s/ but because in Italian loanwords it appears for /tʃ/ (*cello, concerto*). It is even used for /k/ before a front vowel in *Celtic*. Likewise ⟨k⟩ has spread to positions before back vowels in such recent adoptions as *kangaroo* (introduced by Captain Cook, 1770) and in Scottish elements like *kale*, the northern dialect form of *cole* which has replaced the southern word entirely since the eighteenth century. To complete the picture of frustration for those who advocate phonemic spelling, /k/ now appears as ⟨kh⟩ in Eastern borrowings like *khaki* and *khan*, Old English ⟨c⟩ before ⟨w⟩ has become ⟨q⟩ before ⟨u⟩ (*queen, quick*), and French borrowings affected by the change of /kw/ to /k/ in that language have given us ⟨qu⟩ for /k/ in *quay, picturesque*, etc.

a corollary, for ⟨c⟩ also appeared in Old English in the grapheme ⟨sc⟩ which represented /ʃ/, an unambiguous use since the sound sequence /sk/ did not appear in the native language. /sk/ was introduced in Norse loanwords, but since these were largely confined to the eastern areas of England (cf. p. 32), the West Saxon scribal tradition was able to ignore them. The disturbance of the West Saxon tradition and the introduction of some Romance loanwords in /sk/ after the Conquest necessitated change in the orthography if ambiguity were to be avoided, and by the thirteenth century developments parallel to those affecting the representation of /k/ and /tʃ/ may be observed: as ⟨ch⟩ replaced earlier ⟨c⟩, so ⟨sch⟩ replaced ⟨sc⟩. ⟨sch⟩ is the most frequently found expression of /ʃ/ throughout Middle English, being especially favoured in the west midlands consequent upon its use in the AB language, and in some areas of Scotland it remained in use into the sixteenth century. But other graphemes were established in other regional systems, e.g. ⟨ss⟩ in Canterbury and ⟨x⟩ in East Anglia and parts of the north, while ⟨sh⟩ (probably in origin a simplification of ⟨sch⟩, first used by Orm in the east midlands circa 1200, cf. p. 29) gradually found favour in London English at the end of the fourteenth century, was incorporated into chancery spelling, and by 1450 was used for /ʃ/ almost everywhere. The representation of /sk/ in Middle English varied between ⟨sc⟩ and ⟨sk⟩, modern usage being etymological, e.g. words in ⟨sk⟩ are generally of Norse or Dutch origin (from Norse: *skin*, *sky*, *skate* (fish), *skull* (noun); from Dutch: *skate* (verb), *sketch*, *skipper*) and those in ⟨sc⟩ are French (*scarce*, *scorn*, *scullery*) or Greek (*sceptic*, *scope*).[1]

The use of ⟨h⟩ as a diacritic in ⟨ch⟩ and ⟨sh⟩, indicating that ⟨c⟩ and ⟨s⟩ have a pronunciation different from that normally expected of those consonants,[2] was not new to English when ⟨ch⟩ was introduced from French, for ⟨th⟩ had earlier been used alongside ⟨þ⟩ (cf. footnotes to pp. 2 and 17). Both ⟨ch⟩ in French and ⟨th⟩ in English derive from Latin orthography, use of ⟨h⟩ as a diacritic in Latin being made possible by the disappearance of the sounds represented by ⟨h⟩

---

[1] Departures from the etymological principle have ⟨sc⟩ before back vowels and consonants (e.g. Norse *scant*, *scrape*, Dutch *scour*) and ⟨sk⟩ before front vowels (French *skew*, *skim*, Greek *skeleton*). Loanwords from other languages which retain the spelling of the parent language have produced more anomalies, e.g. *school* (educational) and *science* from Latin, *schooner* and *school* (of fish) from Dutch. On the influence of Latin ⟨sc⟩ for /s/ in such native words as *scythe* and *scent*, cf. p. 57–8.

[2] I.e. ⟨h⟩ as a fricative marker, allowing for the fact that ⟨sh⟩ is historically a simplification of ⟨sch⟩.

from the language in the late classical period. As a result of the establishment in English of diacritic ⟨h⟩ in ⟨ch⟩ and ⟨th⟩, other consonant
groups were formed on the same pattern. The grapheme ⟨gh⟩ has
already been discussed (p. 23). ⟨wh⟩ has a rather different history, for
it began in Old English as an initial consonantal combination ⟨hw⟩
corresponding to /xw/. Assimilation of the group to a single voiceless
consonant /ʍ/ had taken place by the late Old English period, and
Middle English scribes, associating the sequence ⟨hw⟩ for the single
phoneme with the use of ⟨h⟩ as a fricative marker in other graphemes,
reversed the graphs to ⟨wh⟩.[1]

English scribes' incorporation into their spelling system of the
grapheme ⟨ch⟩, and the 'consequential' changes which resulted in the
creation of ⟨sh⟩ and ⟨wh⟩, were made possible by their knowledge
of Anglo-Norman conventions. By the fourteenth century, knowledge
in England of continental French facilitated another orthographic
borrowing: the use of ⟨ou⟩ for /u:/. In the preceding century ⟨u⟩ was
a heavily overworked symbol in English. It represented the close back
vowels /u/ and /u:/, and in some areas the close front vowel /y/ (cf.
p. 21). It also appeared for the consonant /v/, because ⟨u⟩ and ⟨v⟩
were not distinguished until the seventeenth century, and frequently
for /w/ before use of the doubled symbol became regular (cf. ⟨u⟩ for
/w/ still in some instances, e.g. *queen, persuade*). Because of this over-
working of ⟨u⟩, the usual Middle English expedient for distinguishing
between a long and a short vowel of the same quality—doubling of the
symbol to denote length—was ambiguous with ⟨u⟩, for /u:/ would
then be represented identically with /uv/, /vu/ and /w/.[2] French ⟨ou⟩
was thus advantageously adopted for /u:/, and though generally the

---

[1] The fricative /x/ also occurred initially before other consonants in early Old
English, /xl, xn, xr/ being represented ⟨hl, hn, hr⟩. Late Old English assimilation of
these groups produced breathed consonants /l̥, n̥, r̥/ which in most dialects fell together
with /l, n, r/ by 1100. Partial survival of /l̥/ in the south-east is suggested by occasional
⟨lh⟩ spellings (e.g. *lhorde* 'lord'). The voicing of /ʍ/ to /w/ is now almost universal in
southern English, though /ʍ/ remains in Scottish dialects and in English speakers
conscious of the spelling ⟨wh⟩. It is remarkable, therefore, that almost all words
with ⟨wh⟩ in Modern English orthography derive from Old English words with ⟨hw⟩
(and conversely that no Old English word in ⟨hw⟩ which survives is represented
other than with ⟨wh⟩). On the few exceptions, cf. p. 58.

[2] Examples of confusion in the thirteenth century are numerous, e.g. the earlier of
the two manuscript versions of the poem *The Owl and the Nightingale* (British Museum
MS Cotton Caligula A ix, second quarter of the century) has *uel* 'skin' and 'well'
uuel(e) and *vule(e)* 'evil', *uele* 'many', *ule* 'owl', *wl(e)* 'foul', where the translations are
necessarily dependent upon the context.

sound has now been diphthongised to RP /aʊ/ (*house, loud, mouth*), ⟨ou⟩ for the long vowel occasionally survives (e.g. in *through, wound*, and French loanwords of the sixteenth century and later: *group, soup*).[1]

It was observed at the beginning of this chapter that by the time of Chaucer's death in 1400 the only living vernacular in England was English. French was widely known, but for the most part it was a foreign language which had to be taught and consciously learnt. Its influence on English, both written and spoken, was thus reduced from that which had existed in the twelfth century, and the French invasion as described in this chapter would have been at an end were it not for the fact that the one area in which Anglo-Norman was still important, the law, was to have a disproportionate influence on the development of orthography. We have seen in the last chapter how important the language used by chancery scribes was in the creation of a national spelling standard. In the same way that the decline of Anglo-Norman as a living language in the thirteenth century caused an enormous shift of vocabulary from that language into English, so the switch from Anglo-Norman to English as the chancery vernacular which occurred about 1430 introduced into English many French orthographic features. But because Anglo-Norman was recorded in England before continental French orthography was stabilised, its spelling was greatly influenced in its early days by the West Saxon scribal tradition. Throughout the three centuries of its existence, Anglo-Norman orthography remained very irregular, and many of the Old English conventions survived in it, alongside French ones. Consequently some of the graphemes which became popular in chancery English in the fifteenth century were English in origin, though they reached what was to become the standard spelling system via Anglo-Norman rather than by direct descent from Old English. For instance, Anglo-Norman scribes took the grapheme ⟨ea⟩ from twelfth-century English to represent the vowel /ɛ:/, and this was returned to English in the fifteenth century. At first it occurred most frequently in words which were common to Anglo-Norman and English, i.e. those borrowed into English from French in the preceding centuries. Use of ⟨ea⟩ in them created the differences which exist today between their representation in the two languages, e.g. *ease, reason*, Mod. Fr. *aise, raison*. (The long

---

[1] From the fourteenth century to the seventeenth, the ⟨ou⟩ spelling is occasionally found to represent the short vowel /u/, later RP /ʌ/, especially before ⟨n⟩, e.g. *doung, wounder*. It survives in *country* (Fr. *contrée*).

vowel is now normally raised to /iː/ in English, but in some words shortening to /e/ has occurred, e.g. *measure, peasant*, Mod. Fr. *mesure, paysan*.)[1] Later ⟨ea⟩ was extended to native words with Middle English /ɛː/, both those which have followed the regular sound development to present-day /iː/, e.g. *deal, meal, meat*, and a number which now have other vowel sounds, e.g. *bread, earth, great, heart.* ⟨ea⟩ was a useful grapheme because it distinguished /ɛː/ from the sound /eː/, a distinction no longer necessary since the two long vowels fell together at the end of the seventeenth century. Anglo-Norman scribes had a number of ways of representing /eː/, and most of them are retained in at least a few words in Modern English. Commonest was the continental French grapheme ⟨ie⟩, which survives in English in French loanwords such as *brief, piece, relief;* this grapheme was so widely used in Anglo-Norman that it has become established in a few words which have never had it in Parisian French (e.g. *chief*), and in the fifteenth century it spread to many native words with /eː/, e.g. *fiend, thief* (OE *feond, þeof*). From Old English orthography Anglo-Norman scribes took the grapheme ⟨eo⟩, and this has become fixed in a few French loanwords (e.g. *people, jeopardy*) which are again spelt differently in Modern French (*peuple, jeu parti* 'divided game').[2] Alongside ⟨ie⟩ and ⟨eo⟩ we have two English graphemes also representing Middle English /eː/, ⟨ee⟩ in words such as *deed, heel, seek*, and the discontinuous grapheme ⟨e-e⟩ in a few words: *here, mere, mete.*

Consonants too were affected by Anglo-Norman contact with English. The sound [x] was lost early in Parisian French but survived in the Anglo-Norman dialect, in part no doubt because of its existence in the English sound-system. Anglo-Norman represented the sound by ⟨gh⟩, an English orthographic development, and the fixing of ⟨gh⟩ for [x] in fifteenth-century London English, out of the very many usages of the day (cf. p. 23), owes much to its use in Anglo-Norman. Even more

---

[1] Old French orthography represented /ɛː/ usually by ⟨ai⟩ or ⟨ei⟩. Both graphemes appear in French loanwords which now have the diphthong /eɪ/ in English, e.g. *plain, saint, reign, feint*, but only the second of them occurs in loanwords which have /iː/ from earlier /ɛː/, e.g. *seize, receive.*

[2] Just as the late Old English sound-change whereby diphthongs were monophthongised caused ⟨ea⟩ to represent /æ(ː)/ in the twelfth century (cf. pp. 12 and 28 footnote 1), so ⟨eo⟩ came to represent a rounded vowel, probably [œ(ː)] or [ø(ː)], at the same period. In some areas this was soon unrounded in English, but the rounded vowel existed in Anglo-Norman in the words cited (and a few others), and was represented by the English grapheme (as well as by other graphemes such as that used in Modern French: ⟨eu⟩).

significant was the Anglo-Norman influence on English consonant doubling. The convention of repeating a consonant to indicate a preceding short vowel, which is so widespread in current English, has a long and complicated history. In part it grew out of a sound simplification of geminate consonants in late Old English, when the double symbol was retained in the traditional spelling system. Similarly, Latin geminate consonants which were simplified in Old French were often represented by medieval scribes with the double symbol which they were familiar with in Classical Latin orthography. Thus in both English and French the convention of using a double symbol to represent a single consonant was well known. The association with preceding short vowels is in origin English, beginning in the late Old English period when long vowels were shortened before a combination of two following consonants.[1] The work of the twelfth-century homilist Orm, whose revised orthography is described on page 29, provides clear evidence that consonant doubling after a short vowel was a recognised feature of English spelling in the period when Anglo-Norman scribes were picking up English conventions.[2] Though consonant doubling remained a sporadic feature of spelling throughout Middle English, it was rarely used with any consistency until the chancery scribes familiar with it in Anglo-Norman reintroduced it to English in the fifteenth-century.[3]

[1] This is a sound-change which may be illustrated conveniently from surviving verb paradigms. In verbs with a long vowel in the present tense, e.g. *feed, mean* (OE *fēdan, mænan*, where ⟨-an⟩ is an infinitival inflection), and with a past tense inflection beginning with a consonant (⟨de⟩ or ⟨te⟩, Mod. E ⟨ed⟩ or ⟨t⟩), the vowel in the past tense was shortened, giving the present-day paradigms *feed, fed; mean, meant* /fiː d, fed; miː n, ment/ (OE past forms *fedde, mænde*).

[2] It should perhaps be noted that the term 'Anglo-Norman scribes' used throughout this chapter means scribes employed in copying Anglo-Norman. It does not indicate either their country of origin or their first language. The fact that the greatest part of extant Anglo-Norman literature was no doubt copied by men whose first language was English explains the considerable English orthographic influence on Anglo-Norman.

[3] In present-day English, mainly because of early seventeenth-century moves towards simplification of double consonants, only ⟨f s l⟩ and ⟨ck⟩ for ⟨kk⟩ are doubled in the final position. Even medially there are anomalies, e.g. *very, city* when compared with *cherry, merry, ditty, witty*. Doubling of ⟨v⟩ (or ⟨u⟩) was impossible in Middle English if ambiguity with ⟨w⟩ was to be avoided, and consequently Modern English spelling does not distinguish vowel length graphically in disyllabic words with medial ⟨v⟩: *lever, never, sever, hover, Dover, rover*, and the only words with ⟨vv⟩ are neologisms formed after the printed word had obviated any possible confusion: *navvy*, an abbreviation of *navigator* in the sense 'excavator' introduced early in the nineteenth century, and other abbreviations which will probably have a shorter life, e.g. *divvy* for *dividend* and the very recent *bovver*, a cant word (variant of *bother* with implied Cockney pronunciation) made current by journalists in 1970.

Not all of the orthographic conventions which were established in fifteenth-century English were of Anglo-Norman origin. London English continued to develop orthographically during the century; ⟨tch⟩ and ⟨dg⟩, for example, replaced earlier ⟨cch⟩ and ⟨gg⟩ for the sounds /tʃ/ and /dʒ/ when medial or final (e.g. in *wretch*, *judge*). (Other features, such as the preference for ⟨v⟩ over ⟨u⟩ for the consonant /v/ will be discussed at appropriate points later in this history.) But Anglo-Norman practice had a significant impact on the emerging English chancery spelling, and it thus provided the last major influence on English orthography consequent upon the French invasion of 1066.

Chapter 4　Renaissance and re-formation

Throughout the Middle Ages, French scribes were very much aware of the derivation of their language from Latin, and there were successive movements in France for the remodelling of spelling on etymological lines. A simple example is *pauvre*, which was written for earlier *povre* in imitation of Latin *pauper*. Such spellings were particularly favoured in legal language, because lawyers' clerks were paid for writing by the inch and superfluous letters provided a useful source of income.[1] Since in France, as in England, conventional spelling grew out of the orthography of the chancery, at the heart of the legal system, many etymological spellings became permanently established. Latin was known and used in England throughout the Middle Ages, and there was a considerable amount of word-borrowing from it into English, particularly in certain registers such as that of theology, but since the greater part of English vocabulary was Germanic, and not Latin-derived, it is not surprising that English scribes were less affected by the etymologising movements than their French counterparts. Anglo-Norman, the dialect from which English derived much of its French vocabulary, was divorced from the mainstream of continental French orthographic developments, and any alteration in the spelling of Romance elements in the vocabulary which occurred in English in the fourteenth century was more likely to spring from attempts to associate Anglo-Norman borrowings with Parisian French words than from a concern with their Latin etymology.[2] Etymologising by reference to

---

[1] The practice of scriveners charging by the inch and adding to their income with superfluous letters seems to have survived in England at least to the end of the sixteenth century; cf. Richard Mulcaster, *The First Part of the Elementarie* (1582), p. 86: 'If words be ouercharged with number of letters, that coms either by couetousnesse in such as sell them by lines, or by ignorance.'

[2] For the most part, changes affected pronunciation as well as spelling, as in the case of *caritep*, a twelfth-century borrowing from Anglo-Norman which later became *charity* (Fr. *charité*)—an instance perhaps of the word being reborrowed from Central French. But more minor changes can be illustrated, e.g. the early borrowing *barun* was

Latin affected English only marginally until the Renaissance thrust the classical language much more positively into the centre of the linguistic arena.

The great revival of learning which swept through the western world at the end of the fifteenth century was centred in a renewed interest in and understanding of the civilisations of Classical Greece and Rome. The fascination exercised by the classics was such that in the first fifty years of the Renaissance—in the period sometimes known as the Age of Humanism—writers and scholars consciously rejected their native language in favour of the Greek and Latin that had proved such subtle instruments in the hands of the 'Ancients'. The enormous expansion of knowledge at the time, the widening of the frontiers of science and philosophy as well as of the boundaries of the known world, created a situation in which the vocabulary of all existing languages seemed insufficient to cope with new demands; there were, as an Elizabethan Englishman exclaimed, more things than words to express things by.[1] Greek and Latin, with their capacity for compounding and derivation, provided the necessary new terms, and these were absorbed into the vernacular languages in the same way that scientific neologisms are absorbed into English today. Humanist writers were so captivated by the flexibility, precision and order of Greek and Latin that the native language was frequently disparaged: 'our language is so rusty' complained John Skelton at the opening of *Philip Sparrow* (c. 1504), where 'rusty' is equivalent to modern 'rustic'. As it was true of the thirteenth century that 'unless a man understand French, people think little of him',[2] so in the sixteenth the ability to read and write Latin was an essential prerequisite of learning. English, having won the battle with French as the spoken vernacular of England in the Middle Ages, spent the sixteenth century proving its capabilities as a written language for the recording of all forms of knowledge and literature. And just as the thirteenth century witnessed the absorption of a large French lexical element into English, so the later period saw an equally great influx of vocabulary from Latin and Greek. As a result both of the increase of Latinate vocabulary in English (and of Greek vocabulary

later spelt *baron* on the Parisian French model. The divergence between Anglo-Norman and Central French spelling has left English with the variant forms *gaol* (Anglo-Norman) and *jail* (Central French).

[1] Ralph Lever, *The Arte of Reason*, 1573, quoted by R. F. Jones, *The Triumph of the English Language*, Stanford 1953.

[2] *Bote a man conne Frenss me telþ of him lute*, Chronicle of Robert of Gloucester.

transcribed in Latin orthography) and of the familiarity of all literate men with Latin, English spelling became as affected by the etymologising process as French had earlier been.

A great many of the learned borrowings from Latin in the Renaissance were doublets of words received into English long before via French, though sound-changes disguised the fact and technical use of the new words gave them more limited application. Thus *pauper* was taken as a legal term direct from the lawyers' phrase *in forma pauperis* and now exists happily alongside *poor*, derived ultimately from the same Latin word (via Old French *povre*). Since *ray*, a Middle English borrowing from French, was particularly associated with light, its Latin antecedent *radius* was borrowed in the more literal sense of a rod or bar, and since *blame*, a thirteenth-century loanword from French, meant 'censure' in a general sense, *blaspheme* was newly taken from the root, Latin *blasphemare*, with the more limited meaning 'revile that which should be sacred'. The fact that these words were doublets was perhaps enough to preserve the original borrowings from being tampered with orthographically, but when the new loanword was related to an existing one, though distinct from it in grammatical function, analogy, the modification of one word on the pattern of another, was liable to occur. For example, from the Latin participle *perfectum* French derived an adjective which passed into Middle English as *perfit*, also spelt in the sixteenth century *parfit*.[1] The Renaissance borrowing into English of *perfection* drew attention to the discrepancy between the English adjective and its classical root, and *perfit/parfit* was respelt *perfect*.

A vast number of medieval French borrowings into English had their spelling similarly revised on etymological lines in the sixteenth century. Not all of the revisions were suggested by related Latinate borrowings like *perfection;* many were simply the result of extreme sensitivity to Latin on the part of writers of English. To take a random sample, *absolve, admonish, captive, corpse, describe, elephant, falcon, language, picture* and *throne* all now have etymological spellings which disguise their descent from the Middle English forms *assoil, amonest, caitif, cors,*

[1] In late Middle English, /e/ before /r/ became /a/, later /ɑ:/. For some centuries words involved in this change were spelt with ⟨er⟩ or ⟨ar⟩ (while, probably, both pronunciations were current). In the seventeenth century, one or other spelling was fixed in most words (for an exception see p. 78), and pronunciation has usually followed the spelling. Words with a discernible Latin etymology were usually fixed in ⟨er⟩ and /ɜ:/ (e.g. *certain, merchant, perfect, servant*), and native words in ⟨ar⟩ and /ɑ:/ (e.g. *dark, far, star, yard*). But ⟨er⟩ and /ɑ:/ have combined (in present-day British English) in *Berkshire, clerk, Derby* and *sergeant*.

descryve, olifaunt, faucon, langage, peynture and *trone*,[1] with consequent detrimental effects on the accessibility of medieval writers like Chaucer to a modern reader. Most of the etymologising was accomplished very shortly before spelling became completely stabilised early in the seventeenth century, and there was thus little time for the pedantic spellings to be lost when the overenthusiastic admiration for Latin declined. On the other hand, the spread of literacy, which accompanied the crystallisation of spelling, offered a new alternative for bringing together sound and symbol. Obviously the more the spelling of a word is fixed, the greater the potential of that spelling as a check on pronunciation will be. With better awareness of the form of the written word among speakers of English in the modern period has come a greater degree of spelling-pronunciation.[2] Hence all the words just cited now have pronunciations based on their reformed spelling, and these serve to emphasise the disparity between their medieval and their modern forms. The spelling-pronunciations did not come into being overnight, and in cases in which the alteration in spelling is comparatively slight it sometimes took many centuries to accomplish the change. Dr Johnson records in his dictionary of 1755 that in the word *fault* (ME *faute*, respelt from the end of the fifteenth century) 'the *l* is sometimes sounded, sometimes mute'; and the etymologised *schedule* (ME *cedule*, pronounced /sedjul/) has gradually acquired two spelling-pronunciations, /sk-/ in American English after form like *scheme* and *school* because that was the pronunciation advocated by Noah Webster in his American dictionary of 1828, and /ʃ-/ in British English after the pronunciation of German borrowings into English late in the eighteenth century such as *meerschaum* and *schnapps*. *Nephew* (ME *nevew*), with the medial consonant historically /v/, is in process of changing to /nefju/ in present-day English pronunciation because ⟨ph⟩ normally corresponds to /f/. Some words have not yet been accorded spelling-pronunciation, the words *choler, debt, doubt, receipt, salmon, sceptre, victuals* retaining the pronunciation better suggested by the Middle English spellings *colere, dette, doute, receite, samon, ceptre,* and *vitailes*.[3] Words of a more literary flavour, e.g. *victuals*, are now occasionally

[1] Middle English forms in this chapter are, unless otherwise stated, those which were used by the best scribes of the early fifteenth century.

[2] Cf. p. 41 footnote 4.

[3] It is worth noting that an accurate spelling-pronunciation of many words of this class would be difficult to achieve in English. For instance, *debt* and *doubt*, on the analogy of *apt* or *clubbed*, might have /pt/ or /bd/ but it is not likely that they could be pronounced /bt/.

heard with a spelling-pronunciation, and condemnation of such pronunciations as ignorant will probably not prevent their ultimate universal acceptance. No doubt such strictures were in the past levelled at /kæptɪv/, /kɔːps/ and /θroʊn/.

As already indicated above (p. 34), an important change overtook the written language towards the end of the fourteenth century: suddenly literacy became more widespread with the advent of cheaper writing materials. In earlier centuries, while parchment was expensive and wax tablets were cumbersome, the church easily retained control of education and writing, but with the introduction of paper, mass literacy became both feasible and desirable. In the fifteenth century, private reading began to replace public recitation, and the resultant demand for books led, during that century, to the development of the printing press. As medieval man ceased pointing to the words with his bookmark as he pronounced them aloud, and turned to silent reading for personal edification and satisfaction, so his attention was concentrated more on the written word as a unit than on the speech sounds represented by its constituent letters. The connotations of the written as opposed to the spoken word grew, and given the emphasis on the classics early in the Renaissance, it was inevitable that writers should try to extend the associations of English words by giving them visual connection with related Latin ones. They may have been influenced too by the fact that Classical Latin spelling was fixed, whereas that of English was still relatively unstable, and the Latinate spellings gave the vernacular an impression of durability. Though the etymologising movement lasted from the fifteenth century to the seventeenth, it was at its height in the first half of the sixteenth. Many of the reformed spellings had very brief lives, and a few have been discarded since. For example, the learned spelling *sanct* (Latin *sanctus*) had a short vogue in England early in the sixteenth century and a rather longer one in Scotland, but *saint* and its early variant *seint* were too strong for it. *Fantasy*, on the other hand, was replaced by the etymologisers with *phantasy* to show its Greek origin, and the ⟨ph⟩ lasted until the nineteenth century when the simpler ⟨f⟩ reasserted itself. Though ⟨ph⟩ is probably quite dead in this word now, *The Authors' and Printers' Dictionary*, which is used as a style-sheet by many publishing houses of the present day, retains the stricture 'not *ph-*' attached to the word, an indication that, in the view of the compiler at least, many people still hesitate over the spelling.

The zeal of those intent on reforming spelling along etymological lines often led them astray in cases in which their knowledge of Latin exceeded that of the history of the words they were emending. Thus *scissors* and *scythe* (ME *sisoures*, *sithe*) were both given inorganic ⟨c⟩ on the assumption that they were related to Latin *scindere* 'cut'; in fact the former derives ultimately from Late Latin *cisorium* 'cutting instrument', and the latter is a Germanic word, Old English *siðe*. In *island* (ME *yland*) ⟨s⟩ was added by association with *isle*, a French loanword derived ultimately from Latin *insula*; the spelling *île* now used in French was the form in which *isle* was first borrowed into Middle English but the sixteenth-century Latinists restored the ⟨s⟩ which corresponded to /s/ lost in pronunciation some centuries earlier. Their extension of it to *island* was unfortunate as this is a native word (OE *ieȝland*), a tautologous compound of *land* with the word for 'island' which survives in many placenames, e.g. *Sheppey* 'sheep-island', *Lindsey* 'the island of Lindon' (Lindon being the old name of Lincoln). Many reformed spellings were the result of false analogy. Because the Old French prefix *a-*, which had developed from Latin *ad-*, was correctly detected in Middle English *aventure* and *avice*, and ⟨d⟩ was restored to give *adventure* and *advice*, a ⟨d⟩ was also added to *advance* and *advantage* (ME *avauncen*, *avauntage*) which ultimately have the Latin prefix *ab-*, and also to *admiral* (ME *amyrel*) which is from Arabic *amir* (cf. Modern English *emir* from the same root). Because Middle English ⟨-au-⟩ was altered to ⟨-al-⟩ (or ⟨-aul-⟩) in many sixteenth-century words by reference to their Latin antecedents (e.g. *balm* and *cauldron*, ultimately Latin *balsamum*,[1] *caldarium*), Middle English *emeraude* was changed to *emerald*, even though there is no ⟨l⟩ in the Latin (ultimately Greek) word from which the Middle English form is derived (*smaragdus*).[2] *Anchor* gained ⟨h⟩ (ME *ancre*) on the supposition that, like *choler* and *echo* (ME *colere*, *ekko*), its origin was Greek.[3] Also with unetymological ⟨h⟩ are *author* and *anthem* (ME *auctor*, *anteme*), the letter having been added on the assumption that, like *apothecary* and *theatre* (ME *apotecarie*, *teatre*), the words are derived from Greek words with ⟨θ⟩.

[1] N.B. the doublet *balsam*, a sixteenth-century borrowing.

[2] ⟨l⟩ in this word is sometimes ascribed to sixteenth-century Spanish influence (cf. Spanish *esmeralda*) since contact with Spain was close in the period, but analogy with the numerous words undergoing the same change seems the more likely explanation.

[3] The ⟨h⟩ is etymologically correct in *anchor* 'recluse', and the semantic association of one 'tied down' to a hermit's cell may have influenced the spelling of *anchor* 'mooring device' which has unetymological ⟨h⟩.

The fact that words with reformed spellings did not immediately —if ever—change their pronunciation introduced many sound-spelling anomalies into English, and paved the way for other changes based on false etymology. Because the etymological spellings *thyme* and *Thomas* retained a pronunciation in /t-/ (cf. ME *tyme*), they suggested the representation of the same sound by ⟨th⟩ in *Anthony* and *Thames*. Because many words beginning with ⟨h⟩ had no aspirate in pronunciation (cf. p. 41), unetymological ⟨h⟩ was introduced into *hermit* and *hostage*, though these, like most other ⟨h⟩-words, now have /h/ in careful speech. Without recourse to an etymological dictionary, few users of English today are able to distinguish between the unetymological ⟨b⟩ in *crumb* and the same letter in *dumb* where it is etymologically correct (OE *dumb*), or the unetymological ⟨c⟩ in *scent* and the etymological one in *scene* and *science*. The writers who first added ⟨b⟩ to *crumb* in the sixteenth century and ⟨c⟩ to *scent* in the seventeenth had no etymological dictionaries to guide them, and their mistakes are therefore comprehensible.

Analogical changes are as natural and inevitable in spelling as they are in other aspects of language, and they have occurred at all stages of the history of English orthography. The use of ⟨o⟩ for ⟨u⟩ in such words as *son* and ⟨c⟩ for ⟨s⟩ in *mice* are analogical spellings, and though these have come into English by its contact with the conventions of other languages, such cross-fertilisation is not a necessary condition of analogy. The majority of analogical changes of the Renaissance period are based on alterations made on etymological principles, but there are some arising from the falling together of phonemes which caused two realisations of a single phoneme to be represented in the traditional spelling of separate words in different ways. This is analogy of the sort that a child may use in writing **nite*, representing the /aɪ/ diphthong of *night* by the discontinuous grapheme of *site*. In the sixteenth century, loss of the sound /l/ in *should* and *would* (due probably to their occurrence in positions of weak sentence stress) led to analogical extension of the retained symbol ⟨l⟩ to another modal verb form *could*, earlier *coude*. All three verbs are inherited from Old English but whereas ⟨l⟩ is historically correct in the first two (OE *sceolde, wolde*) it is inorganic in the last (OE *cuðe*). When /w/ and /ʍ/ fell together in southern dialects of Middle English, the spellings ⟨w⟩ and ⟨wh⟩ were used interchangeably by many scribes, and though ⟨wh⟩ normally survives only in words which had /ʍ/ in Old English (cf. p. 47 footnote 1), it appears unhistorically in *whelk* (OE *weoloc*). By another shift in pronunciation, the labial element of /ʍ/ was lost before /u:/ (represented ⟨o⟩), leaving ⟨wh⟩ corresponding to /h/ in *who, whose, whom*. Consequently from the fifteenth century to the seventeenth, many words with /h/ before a vowel represented ⟨o⟩ had their historic spelling ⟨h-⟩ altered to ⟨wh-⟩, e.g. *whom, whote, whood, whoord* for *home, hot, hood, hoard;* the ⟨w⟩ has survived, without affecting the pronunciation, in *whore* and *whole* (OE *hore* and *hal*). *Whoop*, normally pronounced /hu:p/, is another product of this movement.

It is perhaps significant that these three words with unetymological ⟨w⟩ have homophones in *hoar, hole* and *hoop*. The writings of schoolmasters, which became numerous in English from the end of the sixteenth century, show that conscious efforts were made to avoid homophones becoming homographs also, and many anomalous spellings which have stabilised in English may originate in the desire to remove possible ambiguity from the written language. Such consciousness of the spelling of a word is at the heart of the etymologising reformations of the period. Appreciation of the importance of spelling grew as the sixteenth century progressed, until the diversity of conventions at work in the English system—French, Latin and English—coupled with the increased sound-symbol dichotomy produced by Latinate spellings (spelling-pronunciations following, for the most part, somewhat tardily) led to a questioning of the whole state of the orthography. The Renaissance is thus responsible for two reforming movements in English spelling, etymological reform, particularly in the fifteenth and sixteenth centuries, and phonemic reform, which began in the mid-sixteenth century and has continued almost without pause to the present day. Pressure to reform spelling on a phonemic basis began even before stabilisation, in the form in which we understand it today, was fully completed.

The history of English phonemic spelling reform is traced in some detail in chapter 6, but it is necessary to consider its sixteenth-century beginnings here in order to understand the final stages of the fixing of modern spelling conventions in the seventeenth century. Controversy over reform began in the universities, a prominent Cambridge don, Sir Thomas Smith, producing the first detailed argument in favour of orthographic consistency in a book printed in 1568: *De recta et emendata linguæ anglicæ scriptione dialogus*, etc. Smith's book, as befitted the renowned classical scholarship of its author, was in Latin; so too was the last of the serious attempts at logical discussion of the problems of the orthography to emerge from the first phase of the reform movement, Alexander Gil's *Logonomia Anglica*, published in 1619. In between, writers used English, the two most important books being John Hart's *An Orthographie* (1569) and Richard Mulcaster's *The First Part of the Elementarie* (1582). Hart's work is significant because he was one of the finest phoneticians that English has known. His reform is based on strict phonetic principles, although he recognised at the same time such virtues of traditional spelling as its ability to show etymology or to distinguish between homophones. Mulcaster's distinction lies in the fact that his is the first attempt to marshal the case against reform, though, as we shall see, he was as concerned as the reformers that spelling should be stabilised. In Smith and Hart we find almost all the arguments in favour of phonemic spelling which have since become traditional, while what have become equally conventional appeals for the retention of the existing or traditional forms were made in reply by Mulcaster. Though the reformed spelling system which, according to one modern commentator,[1] most deserved to succeed did not appear until Gil published in 1619, already the decline of the movement was presaged by Mulcaster as he dug the new channel into which the energies of those concerned with orthographic problems were to be directed during the course of the seventeenth century.

A great deal of the interest in reform proposals in the sixteenth century stemmed, as in later periods, from the practical difficulty which schoolteachers found in inculcating the bewildering variety of English spelling conventions, and it was as a teacher that Mulcaster became involved in spelling reform. But Mulcaster was no ordinary schoolmaster. As the first headmaster of the Merchant Taylors' School (where his pupils included the poet Edmund Spenser) and later as High Master of St Paul's School, he became the most famous pedagogue of his day (and for that reason is often assumed to be satirised in the character of Holofernes in *Love's Labour's Lost*). His influence in directing the reform movement is in proportion to his prominence in the teaching world. His book on spelling answers the phoneticians by stating that whereas 'theie appeall to *sound*, as the onelie souerain, and surest leader in the gouernment of writing' (p. 84), he would take account also of what he calls reason and custom. His 'reason' includes analogy within the English system and with those of

[1] Professor E. J. Dobson; cf. p. 96.

other European languages, together with calligraphic considerations such as the decorative effect of the doubling of final ⟨l⟩; 'custom' is traditional spelling which would avoid as frequent alterations in the written language as are observed to occur in the spoken. He says of his own spelling that it is 'as the common, tho more certain then the common' (Dedicatory Epistle). In other words he is content to accept the spelling of his own day but he is concerned to stabilise wherever variant spellings appear. Of particular importance is a *cri de coeur* near the end of the book which calls for the composition of a comprehensive dictionary of the English Language which would be an authority on both spelling and usage. Since the fifteenth century, dictionaries had existed to provide explanations in English of words in Latin and other European languages, and there were also dictionaries from English into French. But no-one had seen the necessity for a dictionary explaining the meanings of English words in the same language. Mulcaster did not live to see the provision of such a work of reference, but as an interim measure he devoted the last fifty-five pages of his book to an alphabetic list of recommended spellings for a large number of words. He tried to blend the principle of phonemic representation ('bycause the letters were inuented to expresse sounds', p. 66) with traditional spelling by preferring for each word the form currently in use which approached nearest to a phonemic spelling, given the conventions of the system as a whole. He was frequently forced to compromise his endeavour to be guided by sound because what he calls custom favoured a flagrantly unphonemic spelling (e.g. *honest*, because 'the originall be well known', p. 194), but he was aware of the desirability of bringing the spoken and written languages into closer alignment, and occasionally he effected some improvement, for example in his proposal for the simplification of some double final consonants: *put, grub, led* for *putt, grubb, ledd*. He seems to have been the first to suggest regularising the use of mute final ⟨e⟩ to indicate vowel length.[1] He also proposed the correction of some false etymological spellings, e.g. he printed *abominable*, correctly derived from *ab-omen-*, rather than the form then current, *abhominable*, which falsely assumes that the second element is Latin *homo* 'man'. As with many of his recommended forms, the proposed change was not fully accepted until long after his death (cf. p. 79); the Shakespeare First Folio, for example, printed more than forty years after *The Elementarie* appeared, has *abhominable* eighteen times but never *abominable*.

[1] Cf. pp. 79–80.

In *The Elementarie* Mulcaster codified existing conventions and formulated rules for learning them. The book, which sprang out of the early reform movement, marks the beginning of the seventeenth-century attempt to simplify the mastering of traditional spelling. If the orthography could not be improved by bringing it into closer association with speech, then at least the teaching of it might be made more certain by ensuring that individual words were always spelt in the same way. With Mulcaster's list of recommended spellings the first step had been taken towards the provision of an authoritative work of reference for spelling, and the stabilisation of English orthography owes more to *The Elementarie* than to all the efforts of those who wished to reform the orthography on scientific lines. Mulcaster's book was a learned work intended for the edification of practising schoolmasters, and though it contained much that was of practical value in the classroom, it was not to be expected that it could be useful to pupils. It was a textbook of education rather than a simple teaching manual, but one which made it possible for someone who had absorbed himself in its educational precepts to produce from them a workbook for the schoolroom. Such a middleman was Edmond Coote, master of the free school of Bury St Edmunds as we are informed by the title-page of his book, *The English Schoole-maister*. The work was first published in 1596 and enjoyed enormous popularity over a long period, the fifty-fourth edition being recorded as late as 1737. Mulcaster's theory is here put to good practical application, though the debt is never actually acknowledged. The rejection of the more extreme propositions of Smith and Hart is brief but firm ('it lieth not in vs to reforme', p. 22), though the use of a dialogue between master and pupil throughout the greater part of the book is sufficiently reminiscent of Smith to suggest that Coote may have known his work well, and the exclusion of information on the 'sounding of the letters' because the subject has been 'before sufficiently and learnedly handled by another' might refer to one of the orthoepists[1] or to Mulcaster. Despite its title, the book is concerned with no part of a schoolmaster's task other than the teaching of reading and writing; it is the first of a spate of spelling-books, or aids for learners, which appeared throughout the seventeenth century and which had considerable influence on the final stabilisation of spelling. Full consideration of Coote's impact is given below (pp. 75–8), but before it can be

---

[1] The concern with pronunciation, common to all the early reformers, has earned them the name of orthoepists.

understood, another thread in the tapestry of English orthography must be examined. During the course of the popularity of Coote's book, English spelling became finally fixed in the form in which we now have it, and though schoolmasters like Mulcaster and Coote played an important part in this final fixing, ultimate responsibility for orthographic developments in English rested then, as now, with the printer. The academic considerations of spelling reformers and the pedagogical concerns of schoolmasters have produced over the centuries many volumes of observations on spelling which range from the high-flown idealism of a Hart to the base pragmatism of a Coote, while the printer through whose hands their very volumes have passed has proceeded along his chosen path with barely an acknowledgement. It is to that path, and the printer's reasons for choosing it, that chapter 5 turns.

6

Chapter 5 The power of the press

Examination of the products of the best manuscript shops operating at the beginning of the fifteenth century shows that professional scribes, men following the trade of scrivener, had already established a large measure of consistency in spelling. The adoption of English as the language of official documents by chancery scribes about 1430 gave scriveners an authoritative standard, and as the fifteenth century progressed so a universal stabilised orthography, in essence that which has become established in English, was increasingly widely used. But whereas the spread of this spelling consistency might have been expected to be helped by William Caxton's setting up of the first English press at the sign of the Red Pale in Westminster in 1476, initially printing proved only a hindrance in the move towards orthographic uniformity. The early printed books produced in England at the end of the fifteenth century are shoddy affairs compared both with the best contemporary continental products (which, though widely available in England at the time, were not in English) and with careful manuscript work. The main advantages that they had over manuscripts were that they were cheap and they could be produced fairly quickly in response to a sudden rise in demand. It is clear that although at first the number of copies produced from a given type-setting was small by modern standards, and though alterations of a minor sort (including spelling changes) might be introduced during a run-off, the possibility of widespread distribution of a stable spelling was much greater with a printed book than with the products of a single scribe, or even of a large scrivener's establishment. But this would depend on the printer using a house-style comparable with that of the manuscript shops, whereas in fact the spelling of most early printed books is very irregular. Rather than further the stabilising movement of the professional scribes, the printers in effect encouraged lack of conformity in spelling.

If ever the time were ripe for the systematising of English spelling,

Figure 2

For asmoche as late by the comaudement of the right
hye & noble princesse my right redoubted Lady /My
Lady Margarete by the grace of god Duchesse of Bourgoyne Brabant &c. I translated a boke out of frenssh in
to Englissh named Reauyel of the histories of Troye/in
Whiche is comprehended how Troye Was thries destroyed
And also the labours & histories of Saturnus, Tytan,
Iubpter, Perseus and Hercules/& other moo than Pey-
hersed. But as to the historie of Jason/towchyng the conqueste of the golden flese/myn auctor hath not sett it in his
boke. but breuely and the cause is for asmoche as he hadde
made before a boke of the hoole lyf of Jason. Whyche he presented Vnto the noble Prynce in his dayes Philipp Duc
of bourgoyne /And also the sayde boke shulde haue ley to
grete. if he had sett the saide historie in his boke. for it con-
teyneth thre bokes beside thistorie of Jason. These for as
moche as this sayd boke is late newe made aparte of alle
thistories of the sayd Jason & the historie of him Whiche
that Dares Frigius & Guido de columpnys Wrote in the
begynnyng of their bokes/ touchyng the conqueste of the
sayd golden flese. by occasion Wherof grewe the cause of the
seconde destruction of the sayd cite of Troye. is not sett in
the sayd boke of Reauyel of thistories of Troye/Therfore
Vnder the protection & suffraunce of the most hyghe puis-
sant & ppen kyng my most dradde naturel liege Lord
Edward by the grace of god kyng of englond and of
Fraunce and lord of Irland/ I entende to translate the
sayd boke of thistories of Jason. folowyng myn auctor
as nygh as I can or may not chaungyng the sentence ne

The Historie of Jason, translated and printed by William Caxton in 1477, opening page
of the translator's preface.

it must seem to us with our hindsight that such a time was at the introduction of printing. But contemporaries could hardly be blamed for failing to realise the potential of their clumsy contraption, and in any case neither Caxton nor any of the other successful early printers was fitted by background or outlook for the role of linguistic reformer. Though Caxton was born in England and had received some elementary schooling in the 1430s, he spent the greater part of his life abroad as an English mercer in the Low Countries. He was clearly an intelligent merchant, for he became prosperous through textiles, and late in life— perhaps in his fifties—realised the trade potential of books and printing. In his hands, printing was a great commercial success, as it was not in those of many of his competitors. His establishment at the Red Pale was primarily a bookshop, the press being an adjunct that was brought into play to supply multiple copies of a proved best-seller at prices much more competitive than those which obtained at manuscript shops. In the operating of his imported machinery, Caxton was obliged to use foreign compositors, and these, unlike well-trained English scribes, were incapable of regularising the spelling of the material they set up in type. Caxton himself seems to have exercised little care either in the choice of good copy or in the supervision of his compositors' spelling. His long years abroad had left him out of touch with fifteenth-century orthographic developments, even had he been alive to such niceties, and his own spelling reflects the patterns he learnt as a boy in the early part of the century. In figure 2 may be seen a sample of his work, the opening page of the prologue he wrote to his translation of *The Historie of Jason*, published in 1477. This is typical in that it shows regular use of ⟨u⟩ for /v/ (whereas the scriveners had established ⟨v⟩ for the sound by 1477, at least in the medial position), and there is no use of the grapheme ⟨ea⟩ (cf. *rehersed, grete, dradde*). Consistency in the spelling of individual words, which had been achieved by the best London scribes of his day, is noticeably lacking in his work; compare, in the limited sample exhibited in figure 2, *hye, hyghe; which, whyche; towchyng, touchyng; hadde, had; saide, sayd, sayde*. In the many translations he made from French, Dutch and Latin, he seems heavily influenced by his sources, the most notorious of his permanent contributions to the language being the introduction of the Dutch convention ⟨gh⟩ for /g/ in *ghost*, a native word spelt *gost* until the later fifteenth century.[1]

---

[1] In Old French orthography, the sound /dʒ/ (Mod. Fr. /ʒ/) was represented ⟨i⟩ (⟨j⟩) before ⟨a o u⟩ and ⟨g⟩ before ⟨e i⟩. The convention was carried into Middle

Such is the debt of English orthography to French and Latin conventions that it is hardly possible to show their special influence on him when translating from works in those languages, but in his Dutch translations, for example in *Reynard the Fox* (1481), there appear very un-English vowel graphemes such as those of *goed* 'good', *roek* 'rook' and *ruymen* 'make room'.

Caxton's press was taken over at his death in 1491 by his assistant, Wynkyn de Worde, and he and Richard Pynson, another Caxton protege, are the most famous printers of the second generation. But it was not to be expected that de Worde, an Alsatian by birth, or Pynson, a Norman, would make any major contribution towards the stabilisation of English spelling, though they did take one step forward by employing English rather than foreign compositors. Caxton and his followers are outside the mainstream scribal tradition, and the usage of the best known early printed books is unrepresentative of the spelling of professional writers of the day. However, during the course of the sixteenth century, as the craft of scrivener was exchanged for that of printer, the orthographic practices of the manuscript shops were transferred to the printing houses, and the products of the best of these reflect the spellings of professional scribes of the fifteenth and sixteenth centuries. A simple example is the use made of the grapheme ⟨ea⟩, taken from Anglo-Norman into chancery English, and increasingly popular with scribes throughout the second half of the fifteenth century (cf. p. 48). Though it disappears almost completely in the work of the early printers, by 1550 it is as fully established in printed material as it was in manuscripts of a century earlier.

The period 1550–1650 saw the universal acceptance by printers of the stable spelling system that with very few modifications is in use today, but the growth and spread of that system was slow and disguised in a number of ways. Most important is the lack of spelling consistency

English in French loanwords, and survives, for example, in *jacket, join, July, germ, giant*. The resulting confusion with ⟨g⟩ for /g/ has sometimes been avoided by extending ⟨j⟩ to positions before ⟨e⟩ and ⟨i⟩, e.g. *jet* (cf. *get*), *jig* (cf. *gig*), or alternatively the French convention of using ⟨gu⟩ for /g/ was adopted (*guess, guide*). In the sixteenth century, ⟨gu⟩ for /g/ was more widespread than it is today (e.g. *guift, guirl* 'gift, girl'), and some printers followed Caxton, whose long association with the Netherlands led him to use ⟨gh⟩ for /g/ very frequently (e.g. *gherle, ghoos, ghes, ghoot* 'girl, goose, geese, goat'). Sixteenth-century books often have ⟨gh⟩ where modern spelling has ⟨gu⟩ (e.g. *ghess, ghest*), and the *Oxford English Dictionary* even records *ghuest*. Sixteenth-century familiarity with Italian literature may have contributed here, as Italian has ⟨gh⟩ for /g/. In English it survives only in *ghost, ghastly* and *gherkin*.

in private writings during the reign of Elizabeth I (1558–1603), which is reflected in many printed books of the period. The irregularity of Elizabethan spelling has frequently been exaggerated. Undoubtedly variation between writers was considerable, but the spelling of well educated individuals, though it might be idiosyncratic, was rarely totally haphazard. Lack of consistency may be put down to the fact that although literacy was fairly widespread, grammar-school education was principally concerned with the study of Latin, and the quality of primary education, which gave the basic ability to read and write English, varied very considerably. Elementary teachers up to 1550 were offered little central direction as regards spelling because they had no textbooks of English and there was no obvious orthographic norm to follow. Printing in the latter half of the sixteenth century was an expanding industry, and many of the houses which came into being produced only poor quality material, set up by compositors with little skill and still less regard for orthographic perfection. They might be expected to follow the irregular spelling of their copy, or make it even less uniform by their own errors. Like Caxton and his contemporaries, they had not benefited from the strict orthographic training of professional scribes. But at the same time there were quality printers who were concerned to ensure orthographic uniformity in their publications, and who established house-styles and trained their compositors to that end. If their works are examined, a fairer assessment of public spelling is arrived at, and the reader can see a gradual extension, from 1550 onwards, of the manuscript tradition founded in the fifteenth century, up to the final fixing of spelling circa 1650.

Once the printers fixed their spelling, a norm was provided for private spelling, and after 1550 we find a gradual improvement in the quality of primary education reflected in greater stability and regularity of spelling in private documents. Representative of a well educated person trained to write in the first half of the century before such regularity appeared is Elizabeth herself. Her spelling may be examined in the many autograph letters which survive, for example in this extract from her extensive correspondence with her successor James I, then James VI of Scotland. The queen is characteristically witty and scornful about James' request for an 'instrument' or guarantee that she will pay his pension.

Tochinge an 'instrument', as your secretarye terme it, that you desiar to haue me signe, I assure you, thogh I can play of some, and haue bine broght up to know musike, yet this disscord wold be so grose as wer not fit for so wel-tuned musicke. Must so great dout be made of fre good wyl, and gift be so mistrusted, that our signe Emanuel must assure? No, my deere brother. Teache your new rawe counselars bettar manner than to aduis you such a paringe of ample meninge. Who shuld doute performance of kinges offer? What dishonor may that be demed? Folowe next your owne nature, for this neuer came out of your shoppe.[1]

The comments are intelligent and the style is mature. The queen's command of the written language cannot be doubted, even though her spelling seems very irregular. Closer examination, however, reveals that although the spelling is not stable, it is for the most part predictable. Like Caxton a hundred years earlier, Elizabeth pays little heed to final ⟨e⟩ or to the doubling of consonants, and consequently her spelling is not consistent: within a few lines appear *musike, musicke, dout, doute*. However, in classical borrowings, where her education gave her an established spelling to follow in Latin, she spells well, even though not always in the way we do now: *instrument, secretarye, performance, dishonor*,[2] and her Latin training perhaps influenced too such features as her apparent fondness for ⟨a⟩ as the unstressed vowel before ⟨r⟩ (cf. *desiar, counselars, bettar*). During the course of her reign an authoritative standard became available for native words as well, so

---

[1] Quoted from *Letters of Queen Elizabeth and King James VI of Scotland*, ed. John Bruce, Camden Society, London 1899. The letter was written early in 1586. James' reply is of interest in showing Scottish spelling of the same period:

> And as for the instrument, quhairunto I desyre youre seale to be affixit, think not, I pray you, that I desire it for any mistrust, for I protest before God that youre simple promeis uolde be more then sufficient to me, if it uaire not that I uoulde haue the quhole worlde to understand hou it pleacith you to honoure me aboue my demeritis, quhich favoure and innumerable otheris, if my euill happ will not permitt [me] by action to acquyte, yett shall I contend by goode meaning to conteruayle the same at her handis, quhome, committing to the Almichties protection, I pray euer to esteeme me,
>
> Hir most beholden and louinge freind and cousin,
> James R.

The continuity of the Scots tradition displayed in the early sixteenth-century Lord's Prayer translation quoted on p. 37 may be seen in the use of ⟨i⟩ in unstressed syllables (*affixit, pleacith, demeritis, otheris, handis*) and as a marker of vowel length (*quhair-* 'where', *uaire* 'were'), and ⟨ch⟩ for /x/ (*Almichties*). One common northern feature not exemplified on p. 37 is ⟨quh⟩ where southern English has ⟨wh⟩ (*quhairunto, quhich, quhome*); phonetically this may suggest an emphasising of the fricative in northern dialects (cf. p. 47), but it is interesting to see the spelling extended here to *quhole* 'whole', which etymologically has ⟨h-⟩ rather than ⟨wh-⟩ and /h-/ not /ʍ-/, cf. p. 59.

[2] Occasional curious errors appear, of the sort that would certainly suggest semi-literacy in a modern writer: e.g. *signe Emanuel* for *sign manual*. (N.B. *manuel* is a perfectly acceptable spelling of the period; it is the confusing of the word with the proper name which is significant.)

that by 1605 the historian William Camden was able to claim in answer to a Welsh critic of the variations of spelling between one Englishman and another: 'it hath beene seene where tenne English writing the same sentence, have all so concurred, that among them all there hath beene no other difference, than the adding, or omitting once or twice of our silent *E*, in the end of some wordes'.[1] Comparison of his spelling and that of the twentieth century makes the claim hardly extravagant.

It was the printers who led the way to the orthographic regularity evident at the end of Elizabeth's reign. One of the best London printers of the period is Richard Field, in whose books we find a spelling both regular and modern. That this uniformity is the product of Field's influence can be shown from one of the two samples of actual printer's copy to survive from the sixteenth century, Sir John Harington's manuscript of his translation of Ariosto's *Orlando Furioso* which was printed by Field in 1591. The manuscript, British Museum Additional MS 18920, has the compositor's marks on it, and was apparently used in the setting up of the printed book. But the spelling of the book is very different from that of the manuscript, as may be seen in the following stanza, the manuscript version on the left, Field's book on the right:

Certes, most noble dames I ame so wrothe,	Certes (most noble Dames) I am so wroth,
with this vyle turke, for this his wycked sinne,	With this vile Turke, for this his wicked sin,
for speaking so great slawnder, & vntroth,	For speaking so great sclander and vntroth,
of that sweet sex, whose grace I fayn would win:	Of that sweet sex, whose grace I fayn would win,
that till soch tyme, hee shall confesse the troth,	That till such time, he shall confess the troth,
and what a damned error, he was in,	And what a damned error he was in:
I shall him make be so in conscyence stownge,	I shall him make be so in conscience stoung,
as hee shall tear his fleshe, and byte his townge.	As he shall teare his flesh, and byte his toung.

Harington, born in 1561 and godson to the queen, displays aristocratic spelling of the early part of Elizabeth's reign. It shows some advance on that of his sovereign, who was almost thirty years his senior, but is

[1] *Remaines concerning Britaine*, pp. 23–4.

archaic compared with that of his printer.[1] Field's spelling probably owes little to his Stratford-upon-Avon origin and grammar-school education; it is the professional spelling of his day, although he is probably a little ahead of most of his fellow-printers in the care and consistency with which it is used.[2]

Even the best Elizabethan printers did not achieve complete regularity in spelling; nor did many of their successors in the seventeenth century. All on occasion made use of common variants. In particular, throughout the period instability is noticeable in a few features: ⟨i⟩ and ⟨y⟩ were interchangeable medially, as were ⟨y⟩, ⟨ie⟩ and ⟨ye⟩ finally; consonants were doubled at random after short vowels; and Camden's final ⟨e⟩ was added without regard to etymology or phonemic representation.[3] These unstable elements alone ensured considerable variety of spelling: pity, pyty, pitie, pytie, pittie, pyttye, etc. During the first two centuries of printing, the primitive machinery available did not allow for the spacing adjustment between and within words which is possible today, and this made type-justification— the creation of an even outer margin—difficult. The earliest printed books are justified in the manner employed by contemporary scriveners: a dash or tilde was used to fill a vacant end-space (cf. figure 2). Later a more satisfactory justification was achieved by varying the spelling of words in a line, and words which had a variable length extending from pity to pyttye became very valuable to the printers. The situation was especially complicated in books in double columns and those containing verse, where the orthography is often more irregular than that of single column prose works because the compositors engaged on them found themselves frequently obliged to alter their regular spelling habits to avoid dividing words at a line end or to fit a verse line

---

[1] With the exception of a single extra final ⟨e⟩, Field's one alteration away from modern spelling is the etymological form sclander, a spelling popular in the period. On the later loss of some etymological spellings, cf. p. 56.

[2] In the Elizabethan age, the printed book was still in competition with manuscripts. In some fields, for example in creative literature, circulation in manuscript was more common than publication in print. For proof that the relationship between authorial and scribal spelling was similar to that between authorial and printer's spelling, cf. The Poems of Sir Philip Sidney, ed. William A. Ringler Jr., Oxford 1962, pp. lx ff.

[3] Instability in these respects has left its mark on present-day spelling. The attitude towards consonant doubling (especially of ⟨l⟩) varies between British and American usage (cf. also p. 86); on ⟨i⟩ and ⟨y⟩ see p. 11 footnote 1, and on final ⟨e⟩ see p. 80. Variation between ⟨y⟩ and ⟨ie⟩ occurs within the paradigm of most nouns ending in ⟨y⟩ (i.e. ⟨y⟩ becomes ⟨ie⟩ before the plural marker ⟨s⟩), and analogy has resulted in occasional singular forms in ⟨ie⟩, e.g. nannie against more usual nanny.

into a printed one. There were other causes of spelling irregularity in the period, for instance the fact that not all printing-houses had a fixed convention laid down by the master printer. In some, discretion was allowed to the individual compositors, and though it is clear that the majority of experienced compositors had fixed habits by 1600, these were not necessarily ones held in common with each other. In normal printing-house practice, more than one craftsman was regularly engaged on the composition of a single book, particularly if it were a large one, and it was even usual for different men to compose facing pages. A brief examination today of a book composed by men with differing spelling habits might suggest more laxity in spelling than was in fact the case with an individual. The first folio edition of the works of Shakespeare, published in 1623,[1] is a book which has been subjected to particularly close scrutiny in the twentieth century, and it happens to be one in which the orthography overall seems to contradict the suggestion that printed spelling was increasingly regular in the early seventeenth century. But it must be realised that it exemplifies all the factors relating to spelling diversity just specified: it is a large book, printed in double columns and containing a large proportion of verse, and it was set up by no less than five compositors, the two principal ones following slightly different spelling conventions. Within the practice of each, Compositor A favoured, for three common words, the spellings *doe*, *goe*, *here*, while Compositor B preferred *do*, *go*, *heere*. Differences in the spelling of these words from one page to the next in the book can usually be attributed to a difference of compositor, but occasionally each 'borrows' the variant favoured by the other for the sake of line-justification. Very occasionally there occurs a totally irregular spelling, and this may sometimes be identified as a copy spelling, introduced perhaps because the compositor was tired or unthinking, or because he had momentarily lost the sense of the material being set up. Such compositorial slips occur sufficiently frequently in late Elizabethan books to be used as evidence of authorship where this is in doubt. Thus although it has been stressed that by 1600 printers were moving towards complete orthographic uniformity, the limitations of their machinery, differences in training and background between compositors, and differences in organisation and outlook between printing houses all militated against spelling being stabilised completely.

[1] *Mr. William Shakespeares Comedies, Histories, and Tragedies.*

The occasional use of variant spellings by an individual was dependent upon more than one spelling of a given word being in regular use.
Only as long as people like First Folio Compositor B regularly used
heere could Compositor A use such a spelling occasionally. Sir William
Craigie, whose work as an editor of the *Oxford English Dictionary* made
him one of the most informed commentators on the development of
English spelling, suggested that the Civil War had an important effect
on the growth of uniformity, printers engaged in the war of words (in
the form of political pamphleteering) which preceded the physical
conflict being induced by the speed at which they were obliged to
work to abandon the varying of spelling for type-justification.[1] This
explains the abandoning by an individual of the variants he used
occasionally, but what it does not explain fully is the printers' adoption,
by the middle of the seventeenth century, of a common system. What
we have to seek are the reasons which persuaded the printers to become
uniform with each other. What finally caused *doe, goe, heere* to be
abandoned in favour of *do, go, here*? An answer favoured by many
linguistic historians is that the printers followed the example set by
the King James Bible in 1611,[2] but the merest glance at that work
shows that its spelling is no more uniform than is that of the Shakespeare
First Folio. In the words of Alfred W. Pollard, published half a century
ago, 'the only consistency is that the form is always preferred which
suits the spacing'.[3] The variant spellings, largely confined to the features
listed at the beginning of the last paragraph, gradually disappeared in
subsequent Authorised Versions in 1629 and 1638, but this was the
effect, not the cause, of increasing spelling stability. For a full understanding of the cause, we must return to the middle of the sixteenth
century and the beginnings of the spelling reform movement.

It is against the background of the printers' practice of making use of
variant spellings and the fairly general disregard of uniformity of
spelling in private writings that the activities of the early phonemic
reformers should be viewed. If they achieved nothing else, writers such
as Smith and Hart made people aware of the deficiencies of English
orthography, and the result was the popularity of spelling books in
the seventeenth century. Though the declared purpose of the spelling

[1] *Some Anomalies of Spelling*, Society for Pure English Tract 59 (1942), p. 307.
[2] The most recent repetition of this argument is by Sir James Pitman in *Alphabets
for English*, ed. W. Haas, Manchester 1969, pp. 47–8.
[3] 'Elizabethan spelling as a literary and bibliographical clue', *The Library* fourth
series 4 (1923–4), p. 6.

books was to help people to learn to spell,[1] the very concept of a 'correct' as against an 'incorrect' spelling which they inculcated had the result of increasing the trend towards uniformity. It is not likely that the academic and scientific considerations which governed the writings of the orthoepists or the pedagogical concerns of Mulcaster and Coote had any direct effect on the printers, for successful printers from Caxton onwards have been primarily businessmen, and their only concern as regards spelling has been to provide their public with what is most acceptable. One sixteenth-century printer, John Allde (active circa 1575–80), did adopt a reformed orthography which attempted to utilise existing conventions in a more systematic and consistent manner,[2] but in general the reform movement passed the printers by. Concern for commercial success led most of them to spell in the manner which the widest cross-section of the book-purchasing public would prefer. An early textbook on the craft of printing, Moxon's *Mechanick Exercises: . . . the Art of Printing* (1683), records that 'it is necessary that a *Compositer* be a good English Schollar at least; and that he know the present traditional *Spelling* of all English Words' (vol. II, p. 193). The seemingly illogical juxtaposition of 'present' and 'traditional' as adjectives qualifying spelling deserves special consideration. Conformity with traditional spelling is an obvious business precaution but the insertion of 'present' suggests an awareness of the changing fashions in spelling; it would appear that to ignore 'present' changes in the generally accepted mode of spelling would be to label oneself old-fashioned and thus to endanger sales. So public taste played some part in the general development of printers' spelling, and it is clear that the schoolmasters and the textbooks they used had some effect on the shaping of that taste. If the books of the reform movement had no lasting influence on either the public or the printer, the spelling books which grew out of them had.

A primitive form of spelling book existed before the reform movement got under way, the earliest surviving example being an *A.b.c. for chyldren* printed in the early 1560s. The genre supplied the needs of children who hoped to reach the grammar school, prospective pupils of which were obliged to have some knowledge of their letters. Sixteenth-century spelling books, as used in the Dame schools and by teaching

---

[1] Cf. p. 88.
[2] Cf. R. C. Alston, 'Bibliography and historical linguistics', *The Library* fifth series 21 (1966), pp. 181–91.

clerks, gave children little more than an ability to say and write their alphabet, until Mulcaster's *The First Part of the Elementarie* attempted to formulate spelling rules, and gave the lead for a more ambitious approach to the subject. As noted briefly on page 62, Edmond Coote's spelling book of 1596 put Mulcaster's precepts into a systematic programmed learning manual, in which the pupil is guided from a knowledge of the alphabet to a capacity for reading the Bible. Even more important than his adaptation of Mulcaster's rules, at least as far as our understanding of the stabilisation of spelling is concerned, is Coote's answering of his preceptor's call for the making of an English dictionary, for in his work, Mulcaster's list of recommended spellings is imitated with one important modification, the addition of a simple gloss to most of the listed words. Mulcaster's desire for a dictionary of universal inclusion was not to be achieved until 1702, with *A New English Dictionary* by J.K. (John Kersey?), but nevertheless this primitive beginning in a book which was to prove of enduring popularity in the seventeenth century fulfilled some part of his intention by ensuring the wide distribution of an authoritative list of 'correct' spellings. Coote limited himself to fewer than 1400 words, those which he considered 'the hardest', and even the meaning attached to these is severely restricted: 'When a word hath two significations, if one be well knowne, I omit that, as to *barke* as a dogge is well known, but a *barke* that is a little Shippe, is not so familiar, therefore I put downe that' (p. 73). But there is some indication of synonyms by means of cross-reference ('*brigantine* see barke') and some primitive etymological guides which show the instincts of a true lexicographer: the use of different type-face to offer a general guide to etymology (Gothic type for native words, e.g. *boat*, Italic for French borrowings, e.g. *bonnet*, and Roman for learned borrowings, e.g. *beatitude*) and the adding of an asterisk to show French borrowings which have undergone some alteration of form in English (e.g. *brandish*, Fr. *brandir*). Figure 3 provides an illustration. Though common words are not included in the alphabetic list, a great many appear as illustrative examples in the earlier chapters, and when it is realised that the book was intended as a manual for teachers and an authority to which pupils might turn for reference, the suitability of the book to fulfil one of the functions that Mulcaster desired of a dictionary becomes clear. An authoritative spelling for the greater part of English vocabulary was available for those who looked for it.

Figure 3

English Schoole-maister. 77

baptifme.
barbarian a rude perfon.
barbatifme barbaroufnes.
barke* fmall fhippe.
barretter a contentious perfo.
barretter allowed to giue counfell
barter* to bargaine.
battrie beating.
baulme
beatitude bleffednes.
beguile.
beneficiall profitable.
beneuolence goodwill.
benigne fauorable.
benignitie bountie.
bereft depriued.
befiege.
biere to carry a dead corps.
bifhope ouerfeer.
blanch* to make white.
blafpheme g. fpeake ill of God.
bloud.
boare.
beaft.
boat.
bough.
bought.
bonnet cap.
bracelet.
bracer.
breefe.
brigandine coate of defence.
brigantine fee barke.
brandifh* to fhake a fword.
broad.

broath.
brothel keeper of a houfe of baudery.
bruife.
bruit.
buggerie coniunction with one of the fame kind.
burgeffe a head man of a towne
build.
calliditie craftines.
capacitie conceipt or receipt.
cancell to vndoe.
canon g. law.
canonife make a faint.
capitall deadly or great.
capable containing.
capitulat.
captious catching.
captiue prifoner.
captiuate make fubiect.
carbuncle k, difeafe or ftone.
carnalitie flefhlines.
cafualitie chaunce.
caftigation chaftifment.
cathedrall gr. church: chiefe in the dioceffe.
catholike g. vniuerfall.
cauldron.
caution warning.
celebrate make famous.
celeftiall heauenly.
catalogue gr. bedroule.
celeritie fwiftnes.
cenfor corrector.
cenfure correction.
centurion captaine.

L 3   ceafe

Edmond Coote's spelling book, 1596.

Coote specifically aimed his book at a wider audience than that of professional teachers and their pupils: he also addressed himself 'vnto such men and women of trades (as Taylors, Weauers, Shop-keepers, Seamsters, and such other) as haue vndertaken the charge of teaching others' (Preface). It was clearly expected that sixteenth-century craftsmen would teach their apprentices not only their trade but also their letters, and the popularity of *The English Schoole-maister* suggests that they found in it an effective textbook. The quotations from the book in the last paragraph and in this show the comparative modernity of his forms, which is another way of saying that the spellings he advocated have in fact been adopted. But though it is easy to put down the general acceptance of his recommendations to the popularity of his book, we are left to seek the source of that popularity. Coote, like Mulcaster, abjured spelling reform, as has been shown (p. 62), but in his adherence to traditional spelling he went further than Mulcaster in his search for the exact 'present traditional' spelling later advocated by Moxon. Marginal alterations in the traditional system resulted from the work of the best of the compilers of spelling books (Mulcaster's *abominable* for *abhominable* being one of them), but where recommendations moved too far or too fast from traditional forms they had no effect. Mulcaster could see no use for the grapheme ⟨oa⟩, which first appeared in English in the mid-sixteenth century and then rapidly and inexplicably found favour with professional writers,[1] and he excluded it as an unnecessary innovation. But when his book was published it had already become part of the 'present traditional' spelling, the printers widely used it, and he was ignored. Coote identified himself much more with the spellings currently in use, and ⟨oa⟩ is firmly ensconced in those words in his list which retain it still. Whereas Mulcaster, the theorist, even though he realised the impracticability of a completely reformed spelling, nevertheless wished to make the orthography more consistent, Coote, the pragmatist, was

---

[1] ⟨oa⟩, which survives in a great many words in present-day English, e.g. *board, boat, coat,* was introduced to distinguish the more open long vowel /ɔ:/ from /o:/, which was represented ⟨oo⟩. Probably ⟨oa⟩ is based on ⟨ea⟩, used at the same period to distinguish /ɛ:/ from /e:/ (⟨ee⟩ or ⟨ie⟩, cf. p. 49). /o:/ has now usually been raised to /u:/ (cf. *soon, moon*) and /ɔ:/ has been diphthongised to /oʊ/, but surviving indication of the earlier correspondence of /ɔ:/ and ⟨oa⟩ may be seen in such words as *broad* and *hoard*. (It should perhaps be noted that ⟨oa⟩ appears briefly in English in the thirteenth century (Henry III's proclamation of 1258) in words which could be spelt either ⟨o⟩ or ⟨a⟩ in the previous century, i.e. those with OE /ɑ:/ or /ã/. There appears to be no connection between this use and the later one.)

concerned to provide a book which would teach children to spell, and also, perhaps more importantly, to read. The teaching of a reformed spelling would lessen a pupil's ability to comprehend material already in print, and the book's popularity and success would suffer. Coote's selection of one particular spelling of each word was motivated therefore not by any of the academic theory which Mulcaster followed but by a concern to have his pupils recognise words as quickly and accurately as possible. Mulcaster's preference for the forms which accorded best with his ideas of 'government by sound, custom and reason' gave way to Coote's selection of that spelling which appeared most frequently in print. Hence it was the printer's spelling which was given authority by inclusion in the spelling book, and the popularity of the spelling book ensured the distribution of a uniform spelling sufficiently widely for public taste to be educated, and for the printers to follow their public. Thus the spelling book and the primitive dictionary, with their growing authority during the seventeenth century, induced the printers to adopt a common orthography.

Mulcaster and Coote were men of the sixteenth century, and complete stabilisation was not achieved in their day or in their books. Mulcaster was forced to retain some doublets (e.g. *perfect, perfit*, cf. p. 54 and footnote 1) because each was equally popular (and, in the case of this example, each was equally phonemic since two pronunciations complemented the two spellings). Coote admitted that 'there are many [words] wherein the best English men in this land are not agreed. As some write *malicious*, deriuing it from *malice*. Other[s] write *malitious*, as from the Latine *malitiosus*' (Preface). In his word-list he prints *malicious*, as Mulcaster had done before him, but the point is made nevertheless. Some of the variants he specified are still available to us, e.g. *jail* and *gaol* (which he prints *Iayle* and *Gaole*), and, if we allow for transatlantic variations, *honor* and *honour*. During the seventeenth century some spelling variants came to be associated, often according to the direction of spelling book compilers, with distinct fields of reference of what is etymologically a single word; for example, *person* 'individual' was distinguished from *parson* 'holder of a benefice', whereas earlier both spellings were used for each of the meanings. Similarly early in the eighteenth century, *flour* 'meal' was distinguished from *flower* 'part of a plant' (Dr Johnson was being old-fashioned in retaining both meanings under the heading *flower* in his dictionary of 1755). In general, successive spelling books of the seventeenth century

record a gradual reduction of the number of variant spellings continuing in use. It is worth speculating on the influence Mulcaster had on
this last phase of the stabilisation of spelling. It has been shown already
that as the virtual founder of English lexicography, Mulcaster played
a most significant part in the development of a fixed spelling convention,
but the earlier part of *The First Part of the Elementarie* is perhaps of equal
importance in the history of orthography because of its enduring
popularity. Its influence was not like that of successful spelling books
like Coote's, with large sales and a wide circulation, for it was intended
for those committed to teaching at a rather higher level than the tradesmen involved in the literacy of their apprentices addressed by Coote.
For nearly a century compilers of new spelling books, though they may
have been influenced by Coote as regards form, looked back to
Mulcaster for ideas, and many recommended changes which he had
proposed long before. His spelling is remarkably modern in his own
day, the greatest discrepancy between his form and ours consisting of
comparatively minor details like the use of final ⟨e⟩ or the appearance
of ⟨ie⟩ where we use ⟨y⟩. Probably the most significant proof of his
enduring popularity amongst the grammar school masters, who had
some success in influencing taste because they were involved in the
education of the more influential literate classes, is the frequency with
which his recommendations were accepted, often long after his death.
For example, forty years before the compositors of the Shakespeare
First Folio were still using varying forms of common words with
comparative freedom, Mulcaster advocated *do, go* and *here*.[1]

One of the most far-reaching changes Mulcaster suggested was for
the use of final unpronounced ⟨e⟩ as a marker of vowel length. Of
the many orthographic indications of a long vowel in English, the one
with the longest history is doubling of the vowel symbol, but this has
never been regularly practised. ⟨a⟩, ⟨i⟩ and ⟨o⟩ were occasionally
doubled in Old English, ⟨e⟩ and ⟨u⟩ more rarely; doubling of ⟨u⟩ was
usually avoided after the introduction of ⟨w⟩ with which it would
have been identical, Middle English /u:/ being indicated by ⟨ou⟩ or

---

[1] About two-thirds of Mulcaster's recommended spellings have been adopted. Only
occasionally do Elizabethan eccentricities appear in his forms, e.g. *akecorn* 'corn of an
ake or *oke*' for *acorn*. It is perhaps significant that some of his efforts have been foiled by
his printer, e.g. the triple ⟨t⟩ in *abuttting* was certainly not intended, and a note
alongside the word *master*, which is listed twice, suggests that one of the two forms
should be the variant spelling *maister*. Many writers of the period ask the reader to
forgive printers' errors overlooked.

7

⟨ow⟩ (cf. p. 47). Double ⟨i⟩ is also rare because of the possibility of confusion with the minims of other characters like ⟨n⟩ or ⟨u⟩. ⟨aa⟩ was common until the fifteenth century in such words as *naam(e)* 'name' and *saam(e)* 'same' but the practice was dropped when the sound represented became diphthongised in the move from Middle English /ɑ:/ towards modern /eɪ/. Use of final ⟨e⟩ as a device for denoting vowel length (especially in monosyllabic words such as *mate, mete, mite, mote, mute*, the stem vowels of which have now usually been diphthongised in Received Pronunciation) has its roots in an eleventh-century sound-change involving the lengthening of short vowels in open syllables of disyllabic words (e.g. /nɑmə/ became /nɑ:mə/). When final unstressed /ə/ ceased to be pronounced after the fourteenth century, /nɑ:mə/, spelt *name*, became /nɑ:m/, and paved the way for the association of mute final ⟨e⟩ in spelling with a preceding long vowel. After the loss of final /ə/ in speech, writers used final ⟨e⟩ in a quite haphazard way;[1] in printed books of the sixteenth century ⟨e⟩ was added to almost every word which would otherwise end in a single consonant, though the fact that it was then apparently felt necessary to indicate a short stem vowel by doubling the consonant (e.g. *bedde, cumme, fludde* 'bed, come, flood') shows that writers already felt that final ⟨e⟩ otherwise indicated a long stem vowel. Mulcaster's proposal was for regularisation of this final ⟨e⟩, and in the seventeenth century its use was gradually restricted to the words in which it still survives. But something of the earlier multiplication of final ⟨e⟩s remains in such modern spellings as *done, gone, have, live, love, doctrine*, with short vowels, and in a large group which have clear indication of the long vowel (or diphthong) without the ⟨e⟩ but which would otherwise end in a consonant or consonant group which in the standardised spelling never stand finally: ⟨z⟩, ⟨v⟩, and ⟨th⟩ for /ð/, e.g. *sneeze, groove, seethe*, and ⟨s⟩ when it is not a plural marker, e.g. *loose*.

By 1700 stabilisation was complete. The relatively few changes which have taken place in spelling since then have affected only a small number of words, for example individual cases like *phantasy* becoming *fantasy* (cf. p. 56) and *controul* becoming *control* (by analogy with French), or minor developments involving a group of words such as the loss of final ⟨k⟩ from ⟨-ick⟩ in such words as *music* and *comic* (cf. p. 85). Perhaps the most far-reaching of late changes was the

[1] Cf. William Camden, quoted on p. 70.

creation of two new graphemes in ⟨v⟩ and ⟨j⟩, used up to the eighteenth century as variant graphs of ⟨u⟩ and ⟨i⟩. As early as the fifteenth century the best scriveners tended to use only ⟨v⟩ for /v/ in medial positions at least, and complete division of the character into the rounded form for vowels and the angular one for consonants was advocated by John Hart in 1569 in *An Orthographie* (cf. p. 94) and by many of the seventeenth-century writers on spelling, but ⟨u⟩ and ⟨v⟩ continued to be treated as one letter alphabetically for a very long time, Charles Richardson's *A New Dictionary of the English Language* published in 1836 still having, for example, the entry *udder* after *vaunt* and before *veal*. The position is exactly comparable with ⟨i⟩ and ⟨j⟩, the earliest division into ⟨i⟩ vowel and ⟨j⟩ consonant occurring in the sixteenth century, and Richardson in 1836 still having the entries *jam, iambic, jangle* in that order.

We have here a useful illustration of the slow response of the public, and more especially of the printers, to the suggestions of the grammarians. English spelling seems to have been particularly resistant to the interference of linguistic philosophers. The situation was quite different in France, where the *Académie française*, founded in 1635, had the specific duty of prescribing on linguistic matters. During the course of the eighteenth century the Academy came to have increasing influence on French orthography through the spelling advocated in the various editions of its dictionary. Though the earliest editions followed the traditional French spelling of the day, the third and fourth (published in 1740 and 1762) introduced a vast number of reforms which revised the spelling of more than a quarter of the entries. Some of the traditional forms were restored in nineteenth-century revisions of the dictionary, but on the whole they have survived, with the Academy dictionary remaining the basic authority on French spelling. England, on the other hand, never achieved an academy, despite the efforts of the Royal Society, of literary men like Dryden, Evelyn and Swift, and even of the Government who gave the proposal their backing in 1712. No British Academy was formed and no academic dictionary appeared to revise the orthography which was standardised in the seventeenth century.[1]

[1] The attempt to impose some academic authority on spelling continues today. Compare the call by Emeritus Professor Simeon Potter in *Changing English* (London 1969, p. 47) for the collaboration of scholars in Britain and the United States 'in the production of a dictionary of approved spellings, not static and sacrosanct, but progressive and forward-looking, and subjected to (not too frequent) revisions'.

The eighteenth century did nevertheless see the creation of a most important *Dictionary of the English Language*, that published by Samuel Johnson in 1755. Johnson's dictionary cannot be praised too highly. Its distinction lies in the quality of writing introduced to the form rather than in any new direction given to lexicography, for it aimed only at logical extensions to developments already started in Nathaniel Bailey's *An Universal Etymological English Dictionary* of 1721 (an interleaved copy of which Johnson used as the basis for his own work). But the fact that the significations are by an urbane and wise writer with a wide vocabulary and a fine command of style raised the work far beyond the status of a mere reference book, and the enormous authority with which its statements were made, however wrong, ensured for it a well deserved popularity. Throughout the nineteenth century no home of a literate Englishman was complete without, alongside the Bible and the works of Shakespeare, a copy of *The Dictionary*, and its authority has been so great that we may forgive the many writers of our own day who have assumed that Johnson is responsible for the anomalies of English spelling. But the truth is that Johnson was powerless to do more than record the already established convention. As he admitted in his Preface: 'I have often been obliged to sacrifice uniformity to custom; thus I write, in compliance with a numberless majority, *convey* and *inveigh*, *deceit* and *receipt*, *fancy* and *phantom.*' Spelling, at least the public spelling of the printers, was already firmly fixed, and, large as the figure of Samuel Johnson in the history of English letters undoubtedly is, in the development of spelling he had almost no influence at all. What is of significance is that, like the French Academy dictionaries almost contemporary with his, Johnson's dictionary became the accepted standard for *private* spelling during the nineteenth century, and since he followed the printers, Johnson is responsible for the establishment of printers' spelling in private use.

So far in this history there has been little reference to the fact that English today is a world language, and no account of orthographic practice outside Great Britain. In the future the development of British spelling may be affected by the fact that the language is now used as mother tongue or second language by peoples all over the world, but as yet only one orthography has appeared outside Britain which has had significant impact on the spelling of Standard English. This is the spelling generally (though not universally) used in the United States of

America, and in order to understand such differences as there are between American and British spelling we must now turn to the life and works of another lexicographer, one whose popularity in his own country is comparable with Johnson's in Britain: Noah Webster.

Webster's first book, *A Grammatical Institute of the English Language*, published in 1783 when he was only 25, was a spelling book aimed at providing the newly autonomous American states with their own school textbook, and ensuring their independence in the study of grammar as in other fields. The fact that by the time of his death sixty years later the book had been reissued (under the title *The American Spelling Book*) some four hundred times indicates its success. In this first book, Webster specifically stated that he followed Johnson's spelling, and he castigated attempts at both partial and complete reform. For example, of those who would drop the ⟨u⟩ from *honour* and *favour* he stated: 'it happens unluckily that, in these words, they have dropped the wrong letter—they have omitted the letter that is sounded and retained one that is silent; for the words are pronounced *onur*, *favur*' (p. 11, footnote). Curiously enough, with the profits from his conservative spelling book he launched into the reform business, publishing a call for a most radical alteration of the traditional system in *Dissertations on the English Language* only six years afterwards in 1789. Though later in life he withdrew from this extreme position, a number of his reformed spellings remained enshrined in his most famous work, *An American Dictionary of the English Language* (1828), those spellings which most present-day users of British English regard as Americanisms stemming from this dictionary. It is ironical that the very spellings he so roundly rejected in early life, *honor* and *favor* (probably the most easily identifiable of American spellings today), have become established in American usage because of his inclusion of them in his dictionary.[1]

The suggestion that Webster's advocacy of some reformed spellings in his dictionary is responsible for the spread of such spellings leads to the inference that Webster had more success in influencing the development of American usage than Johnson had with British usage. Such a conclusion needs careful qualification. By the nineteenth century, the dictionary had taken the place of the seventeenth-century spelling book as the recorder of the spellings most generally favoured by printing

[1] Use of ⟨or⟩ rather than ⟨our⟩ in such words was maintained by a small minority of printers in Britain up to the time of the publication of Webster's dictionary. Not until the twentieth century did such spellings become firmly associated with American usage.

houses. Like Johnson, Webster could record only those spellings already widely used by printers, and, again like Johnson, his greatest influence was on the private speller who found in his dictionary a reference book to currently acceptable spelling. Unlike Johnson, however, but like Mulcaster two centuries earlier, Webster deliberately chose from the spellings to be found in printed material of his day not simply the commonest spelling of a particular word but the one which accorded best with his orthographical theories. He was able to do so because American public spelling was rather more fluid than British spelling in Johnson's day, 'authorised' spelling of the reference books having a somewhat slighter hold on American printers and their public. Webster's choice was guided not just by the usual considerations of reformers (cf. chapter 6) but also by the desire to make American spelling distinct from British spelling, a concern which sprang from his intense nationalism. Most of the revised spellings advocated in his reform proposals could not be included in the dictionary because there was no authority for them in current printing practice, but he did include some for which there seemed slight justification.[1] Many of these were discarded in subsequent editions of the dictionary, by Webster himself in the second edition printed two years before he died in 1843, and in the second half of the nineteenth century by later editors, concerned to ensure the continued popularity and authority of what had become a standard reference book. But some remained, and since the book was successful in establishing its authority throughout the States, they have become generally recognised as American forms. In the sense that Webster was the first to differentiate between British and American usage, and in that it was frequently he who chose the variant of two spellings in early nineteenth-century use which has subsequently been preferred in the United States, he can be said to have influenced the development of spelling. He is in a way 'responsible' for such forms as *center, color* and *defense*.

Minor changes in spelling continued to be recorded in dictionaries on both sides of the Atlantic throughout the nineteenth century. By and large these reflected a change of emphasis in the choice between alternative spellings which were hangovers of an earlier period of

---

[1] In a very few instances Webster recommended a spelling not generally in use but one which he felt was justified etymologically. For example, under MOLD he wrote: 'the prevalent spelling is MOULD; but as the *u* has been omitted in the other words of this class, as *bold, gold, old, cold*, etc, it seems desirable to complete the analogy by dropping it in this word'.

greater spelling freedom. *Phantasy* was rejected in favour of *fantasy*, for example, both having been equally common since the sixteenth century (cf. p. 56). Webster's zeal for differentiation and for change often caused American spelling to be ahead of British usage, but, for a while at least, parallel developments were observable in the two systems. Thus Webster's omission of final ⟨k⟩ in *musick, publick*, etc. became general in Britain later in the nineteenth century (though ⟨k⟩ remains before a bound morpheme: *havocking, panicked*.) There are still available a surprisingly large number of words with more than one currently acceptable spelling, at least according to the dictionaries, though narrowing of this choice is a continuing process. It is difficult to pinpoint precisely the responsibility for the loss of a spelling variant in the modern period, but of greatest influence is certainly the printer, as this chapter has repeatedly emphasised; with notable exceptions like Webster, the philologist and the lexicographer have had little or no impact. For example, from the Middle Ages the two spellings *gray* and *grey* have been equally acceptable. Johnson recorded a preference for *gray* and dictionaries throughout the nineteenth century followed his example, but by the end of that century only *The Times* of the more important British publishing organisations retained it. *Grey* is now universal in Britain and *gray* regarded as transatlantic. The first volume of the *Oxford English Dictionary*[1] made a special plea for *ax* as the spelling of *axe* but again in Britain it was ignored, though in the United States it survives because Webster preferred it. Chauvinism in the twentieth century has tended to reduce the impact of American spellings on British publishers but comparatively rare words continue to be affected. In the last twenty years or so, British printers have come to accept the American simplification of the ⟨ae⟩ and ⟨oe⟩ digraphs (or ligatures) in classical borrowings such as *encyclopedia, medieval, fetid*, though many survive, e.g. *archaeology, Caesar*. The process of change can often be observed by comparison of the practice of the 'serious' newspapers with that of the 'popular' ones, for instance the *Daily Express* style-sheet current at the time of writing of this chapter specifies the spelling *hemorrhage*, while that for *The Guardian* has the more conservative *haemorrhage*. Changes which involve the shortening of a word have become increasingly noticeable in the twentieth century. Printers in

---

[1] Published as *A New English Dictionary on Historical Principles*, first fascicule 1884, first volume 1888. The title *Oxford English Dictionary* first appeared on the reprint of 1933.

particular are attracted by the appreciable savings in production costs to be made by the use of spellings which economise in space. Essentially it was the reforming instinct of Noah Webster which caused most distinctively American spellings to be briefer than their British counterparts, and despite the still widespread dislike of American forms prevalent in Britain,[1] it is likely that publishers will be unable ultimately to resist the saving in paper, ink, and type-setting labour involved in the shortened forms *catalog* and *program* against *catalogue* and *programme*. As books and periodicals published in the United States become increasingly familiar in Britain, American spellings are inevitably becoming more difficult to detect. The ability of sub-editors, publishers' readers and compositors to regularise American-influenced copy to the British standard is already suffering, British reprints of American novels, for example, having many examples of the overlapping of the two orthographies, and the style-sheets of some scientific publishers have already absorbed *catalog* and *program*. Brevity is the keynote of present developments in spelling. Fully established in the style-sheets now are *loth* against *loath*, *curtsy* against *curtsey*, *hiccup* against *hiccough*, *biased* and *focused* against *biassed* and *focussed*. Comparison between popular and serious newspapers again shows this process at work: against the *Daily Express dulness* and *fulness*, *The Guardian* has *dullness* and *fullness*.

Printers' style-sheets may thus be seen to be of fundamental importance in the establishment of current spelling trends. Since most British publishers base their house styles on *Chambers' Twentieth Century Dictionary*, it might be claimed that the compilers of that work have a not inconsiderable authority and potential for change.[2] But *Chambers'* is used simply because it is the British dictionary most frequently revised and therefore most responsive to present-day usage, and we are faced again with the circular process of the printer relying on the authority of the word-list which in turn is based on printers' usage—the circumstances which led to spelling stabilisation in the seventeenth century. Inevitably *Chambers'* is occasionally left behind by the printers. The latest edition (published 28 April 1972) recom-

---

[1] It is interesting to note a reversal of the nineteenth-century position, when Americans such as Webster were anxious to avoid British forms. The use of definably British spellings in America seems not to disturb Americans today.

[2] Also important are two style-sheets generally available: *The Authors' and Printers' Dictionary* by F. Howard Collins, first published in 1905 and frequently revised by Oxford University Press; and *Rules for Compositors and Readers at the University Press, Oxford* by Horace Hart, first published 1893 and now in its thirty-seventh edition.

mends the spelling *dietitian*. This, though etymologically incorrect, is the form in which the word was first recorded in *The Fortnightly Review* in 1846, and subsequently lexicographers in Britain and America have kept to it. But *dietician* has long been favoured by writers conscious of the analogy of *optician, physician,* etc, and it seems likely that this is the form of the future. Though *The Guardian's* style-sheet retains *dietitian* for the moment, the *Daily Express* adopted *dietician* before the 1972 edition of *Chambers'* was published.

A development which may in time be of significance should be noted in the latest authoritative American dictionary to appear, *Webster's Third New International Dictionary of the English Language*, published in 1961. True to its role as a recorder, the dictionary includes as part of the 'identification' of many of the entries variant spellings which are usually classed as ignorant or incorrect. The practice may easily be justified, for such common departures from traditional spelling as *caligraphy, ecstacy, idiosyncracy, supercede* and *surprize* have a rightful place in a list of forms which are undoubtedly encountered today in both written and printed matter. Less easy to justify is the fact that each of these spellings is recorded as what the introductory material of the dictionary calls a 'secondary variant belong[ing] to standard usage and . . . for personal or regional reasons . . . preferred by some' (p. 16a, §1.7.2). Certainly the forms listed above have not, until recently, been part of 'standard usage', but the very inclusion of them in an accepted work of reference may ultimately have the effect of establishing their currency in received standard usage.

Chapter 6 Sound spelling

This chapter is concerned with manifestations of two basic attitudes to spelling over the centuries: the condemnation of departures from the conventional spelling system by those who see rigid adherence to it as a mark of full literacy, and the dissatisfaction with traditional orthography associated with the search for an optimal writing system for English. Though the two are not unconnected, since many of those who have been concerned to revise spelling have wished to do so in order that literacy might be achieved and maintained more easily, the views are so opposed at their extremes that it is better to review the expression of each in separate chronological sequences.

Public censure of the bad speller has a long history. It is implicit in the preface to Coote's *English Schoole-maister* of 1596 in the remark:

I undertake to teach all my scholers, that shall be trayned up for any grammar schoole, that they shall neuer erre in writing the true orthography of any word truly pronounced . . . and the same profit doe I offer vnto all other both men & women, that now for want hereof are ashamed to write vnto their best friends: for which I haue heard many gentlewomen offer much.

Spelling book writers through the history of the genre in the seventeenth century commend their works to adults in similar fashion. Thomas Lye addressed *A New Spelling Book* in 1677 not only to children but to 'persons of riper Age' of whom it might be said: '*Read*, they hope they can; but *spell* they cannot; and therefore to *write* either to Child, Friend, or Servant, they are ashamed'. The denotation of social class is clear; people ashamed to write to servants are undoubtedly themselves employers of servants, and bad spelling is thus not confined to the poorer members of society whose education might reasonably be expected to have been slight.

The universal response to incorrect spelling was laughter, and it was the fear of such ridicule that the spelling book writers relied on to produce their adult audience. The educational shortcomings of the bad speller and the merriment his mistakes provoked were expressed by William Holder in *Elements of Speech* (1669): 'we are apt . . . to laugh at the uncouth Spelling in the writings of unlearned persons, who writing as they please, that is, using such Letters, as justly express the power or Sound of their Speech; yet, forsooth, we say write not *true English*' (p. 107). Holder is not satisfied with this general response, for his claim is that the fault lies in the spelling system (for not being accommodated to pronunciation) rather than in those who wrongly represent it, but he could not alter society's attitude, and its amusement at the expense of those incapable of orthographic conformity continued unchecked. Though Coote mentions 'both men & women' in his preface, it is the latter who he feels will find his book particularly valuable. Jokes on the inability of women to spell correctly are not uncommon in literature of the seventeenth and eighteenth centuries. Typical of the period is a wry comment in an early issue of Sir Richard Steele's short-lived periodical *The Guardian* (28 March 1713); remarking on a sheet of poetry discovered by chance, the writer says:

> By the Hand, at first sight, I could not guess whether they came from a Beau or a Lady, but having put on my spectacles, and perused them carefully, I found by some peculiar Modes in Spelling, and a certain Negligence in Grammar, that it was a Female Sonnet.

The quotation from Holder shows that bad education was usually held to be the cause of poor spelling ability, and since women were worse educated in the main than their male social counterparts, it was hardly surprising that they should find the art of spelling a difficult one to acquire. Jonathan Swift is quite explicit in his *A Letter to a Young Lady on her Marriage* (published in 1727):

> It is a little hard that not one Gentleman's daughter in a thousand should be brought to read or understand her own natural tongue, or be judge of the easiest Books that are written in it: . . . and it is no wonder, when they are not so much as taught to spell in their childhood, nor can ever attain to it in their whole lives.

It should be noted that *spell* here has the simple sense 'read' (now obsolescent) rather than the current meaning of knowing the separate letters of a word. Swift is suggesting general illiteracy among women rather than mere failure to conform to the accepted spelling norm, but if we allow for the exaggeration of the satirist, the main point of the inadequacy of the education of women of all ranks is made. However, although many of the serious comments on spelling were aimed at women, while the wags had great fun at their expense too, a more complete picture of the importance that had come to be attached to conformity in spelling may be drawn from attacks on the occasional slips perpetrated by men. Lord Chesterfield, well known for his series of letters on the conduct of a gentleman addressed to his son, made clear the general condemnation occasional orthographic error might excite in a letter dated 19 November 1750:

I come now to another part of your letter, which is the orthography, if I may call bad spelling *orthography*. You spell induce, *enduce;* and grandeur, you spell *grandure;* two faults, of which few of my house-maids would have been guilty. I must tell you, that orthography, in the true sense of the word, is so absolutely necessary for a man of letters, or a gentleman, that one false spelling may fix a ridicule upon him for the rest of his life; and I know a man of quality, who never recovered the ridicule of having spelled *wholesome* without the *w*.

Chesterfield certainly exaggerated the literary capabilities of his house-maids, for adherence to the printers' norm in spelling was the aim rather than the achievement of his contemporaries, as private documents of the period demonstrate.[1] Not content with mere censure, however, he moved on to some practical advice for his son on how correct spelling might be attained.

Reading with care will secure everybody from false spelling; for books are always well spelled, according to the orthography of the times. Some words are indeed doubtful, being spelled differently by different authors of equal authority, but those are few; and in those cases every man has his option, because he may plead his authority either way; but where there is but one right way, as in the two words above-mentioned, it is unpardonable and ridiculous for a gentleman to miss it: even a woman of tolerable education would despise, and laugh at a lover, who should send her an ill-spelled *billet-doux*.

It is interesting to note that no mention is made here of a reference book for spelling, other than the printed book generally. A number of dictionaries were available, but their authority in private spelling was not established until after the appearance of Johnson's work in 1755. By the end of the century, cure for spelling ills could be placed firmly

---

[1] Chesterfield elsewhere shows his awareness of the fact that what he calls misspelling is a common feature of the writing of both sexes; compare his comments on Johnson's projected dictionary in *The World* 5 December 1754: 'I . . . most earnestly recommend to my fair countrywomen, and to their faithful or faithless servants, the fine gentlemen of this realm, to surrender, as well for their own private as for the public utility, all their natural rights and privileges of misspelling, which they have so long enjoyed, and so vigorously exerted'.

in the dictionary. A manual of correct letter-writing, maintaining that spelling was 'of the highest importance' in the art, states:

Ignorance in this particular is always considered a mark of ill-breeding, defective education, or natural stupidity. To attain [correct spelling] it is necessary to observe the method followed by the best writers of the present day, and to consult some good modern Dictionary.[1]

A comparison between the fixed form of the written language and the relative laxity in the spoken was made by Thomas Sheridan in *A Course of Lectures on Elocution* in 1763:

It is a disgrace to a gentleman, to be guilty of false spelling, either by omitting, changing, or adding letters contrary to custom; and yet it shall be no disgrace to omit letters, or even syllables in speaking, and to huddle his words so together, as to render them utterly unintelligible.[2]

Sheridan deduced that the reason for the discrepancy is that 'the written language is taught by rule, and it is thought a shame for any one, to transgress the known rules of an art, in which he has been instructed', but he doubted the wisdom of the distinction, for writing may be examined at leisure, the reader supplying 'any defects of orthography', whereas this is not the case with speech. Since elocution was Sheridan's main concern, his observations on spelling are made only in passing, but they highlight the principal eighteenth-century attitudes: spelling should be learnt by rule, and departure from the rule is a sign of ignorance. The same views have persisted to the present day, but whereas in the eighteenth century such signs of ignorance attracted only ridicule, in the nineteenth, as the modern emphasis on qualification by examination came into being, the bad speller might find his livelihood threatened by his disability. Towards the end of the century, spelling reformers on both sides of the Atlantic were fond of quoting a remark by Dr Morell, a famous Inspector of Schools in England, that 'out of 1,972 failures in the Civil Service examinations, 1,866 candidates were *plucked for spelling*. That is, eighteen out of every nineteen who failed, failed in Spelling.'[3] The educational system in the nineteenth century set such store by spelling that, according to one transatlantic

---

[1] *The London Universal Letter-Writer*, c. 1800, p. 1.
[2] Lecture II, p. 40.
[3] First quoted in Pamphlet 330 of The Reading, Writing, and Spelling Reform, 1877, p. 16; the italics are presumably introduced by the editor, Isaac Pitman; cf. p. 106 below.

schoolmaster,[1] the whole syllabus seemed designed only to teach the single key to all knowledge:

Our children spell their way laboriously, carefully, tearfully, many times, through the eight grades of the primary and grammar schools, completing something every here and there, but never the spelling. Entering the High Schools, they find it there in every year of the course—twelve years for the course in spelling—spelling everywhere and everywhen; spelling oral and written; spelling singly and in classes; spelling solo and in concert; spelling from card and from speller; spelling from readers First, Second, Third, Fourth, and Fifth; spelling from text-books in arithmetic, grammar, geography, and history; and, in addition to all this, long lists of selected words are placed upon the blackboards for no other purpose than that their spelling may be memorized. Then after leaving school, there must needs be an occasional revival of the old-fashioned spelling school, in which the participants spell at a mark or prize, to stimulate further study in the orthographic art.

It is necessary to allow here for the polemics of the spelling reform debate, in which one side has long maintained that the teaching of reading is unnecessarily hindered by the anomalies of traditional orthography, and that such teaching consequently looms too large in the curriculum. Nevertheless it must be admitted that behind this colourful magnification lies a basically true picture. Our educational system does lay considerable emphasis on the teaching of correct spelling, and the continuing popularity of spelling bees and of spelling questions in general knowledge tests (for example in the BBC's 'Brain of Britain' series) shows that the ability to memorise the traditional spelling of printed books is widely believed to be a mark of full education. The corollary that inability to reproduce the printers' spellings is a sign of incomplete or unsuccessful education is still also very generally accepted, and in our own day spelling errors have been used as ammunition in an education war. The efficacy of 'modern' educational methods was questioned on the grounds that they lead to an imperfect apprehension of correct spelling in the first of the notorious Black Papers on Education,[2] the editors stating:

It is our belief that disastrous mistakes are being made in modern education, and that an urgent reappraisal is required of the assumptions on which 'progressive' ideas, now in the ascendant, are based. Even at the most obvious level, students do not *know* as much as they should: and this despite the much publicised examination grind. A successful business man who had left school

[1] George D. Broomell, lecturing to the Principals' Association, Chicago, 1877; printed as Pamphlet 333 of The Reading, Writing, and Spelling Reform.
[2] *Fight for Education*, ed. C. B. Cox and A. E. Dyson, 1969.

at fourteen recently expressed his surprise that when he hired graduate staff with honours degrees in English he sometimes had to teach them how to put sentences together and spell. An external examiner of Colleges of education writes that it is common to find many students who write 'his' for 'is', who do not know the difference between 'their' and 'there' or 'where' and 'were', who cannot punctuate and cannot spell.

The polemics here are as strong as in the spelling reformer's passage just quoted, and they are dependent in part on 'bad spelling' being an emotive phrase. The conclusion is that the situation of 1596 has not changed: society condemns those who 'erre in writing the true orthography'.

Attempts to improve the writing system the learning of which continues to give so much trouble have been many and various. Interest in the reform of English spelling began strangely enough with a sixteenth-century controversy over the correct pronunciation of Ancient Greek initiated by the Humanist scholar Erasmus. Two Cambridge dons, Sir John Cheke (1514–57) and Sir Thomas Smith (1513–77), adopted the revised pronunciation of Greek advocated by Erasmus on the assumption that the spelling of Classical Greek was phonemic, whereas the pronunciation commonly used in early six-teenth-century schools was that of the Greece of the day, a pro-nunciation which was far from having a one-to-one relationship with Ancient Greek orthography. The development of the controversy at Cambridge is important to us here only in as far as it caused Cheke and Smith to question the efficiency of English orthography, with the result that Cheke adopted a partially regularised spelling of his own devising in his unpublished writings,[1] and Smith wrote the first printed proposal for English spelling reform, *De recta et emendata linguæ anglicæ scriptione dialogus* (published in 1568). The book begins with a reasoned argument in favour of reform. Briefly summarised, it maintains that writing imitates speech, and letters reflect sounds; as different languages

---

[1] Some examples of Cheke's regularisations were available in sixteenth-century printed books, e.g. a letter written by him to Sir Thomas Hoby was printed at the end of the 1561 edition of the latter's translation of Castiglione's *Il Cortegiano* (*The Courtier*). Knowledge of Cheke's practice thus reached later reformers. Thomas Whythorne, for example, notes it in his introduction to his own orthographic innovations recorded in a manuscript dated c. 1576 (cf. Rupert E. Palmer Jr., *Thomas Whythorne's Speech*, Anglistica vol. xvi, Copenhagen 1969, pp. 19–20). Mention of Whythorne gives an opportunity to observe that not all those who have written on the subject of spelling reform can be included in this survey of the movement; only the more prominent or influential are listed. Whythorne himself is largely dependent on John Hart.

have different sound systems, so they need somewhat different alphabets. English needs an extended Latin alphabet to cope with its sound system, and Smith offered new symbols drawn from Greek, from earlier English, and from his own imagination, together with a series of diacritics. In particular, he was anxious to record vowels accurately, and to provide single symbols for the traditional graphemes which involved ⟨h⟩: ⟨ch⟩, ⟨gh⟩, ⟨sh⟩, ⟨th⟩, ⟨wh⟩. As a phonetician he was soon surpassed, and his arguments for reform and his reformed system itself were later much improved upon, but his book continued to be read and quoted by linguists for more than two centuries.

John Hart, of whom we know very little except that he describes himself as 'Chester Herald', published in 1569 *An Orthographie*, the first proposal for spelling reform to be printed in English. Both he and Smith observe in their respective prefaces that they had contemplated the state of the orthography for a long time, and a surviving manuscript draft of Hart's book dated 1551 (British Museum MS Royal 17 C vii) not only supports his statement but provides us with the earliest extant treatise on English spelling. As Smith was influenced by the controversy over Greek, Hart was stimulated by an attempt to reform French orthography on phonemic lines, Loys Meigret's *Traité touchant le commun usage de l'escriture* (1545), referred to on page 53 of *An Orthographie*. Hart's alphabet is more practical than Smith's, avoiding some of the latter's dependence on diacritics, and its value is the greater because its inventor was a better phonetician. Like Smith, he created new letters and excluded some existing ones (both would excise ⟨c⟩, Smith avoids ⟨q⟩ and Hart ⟨w⟩ and ⟨y⟩). Recognising the value of traditional spelling in showing etymology and distinguishing between homophones, Hart nevertheless maintained that such was the confusion and disorder of spelling 'as it may be accounted rather a kinde of ciphring, or such a dark kinde of writing' (p. 2), and that a one-to-one correspondence with sounds was in every way preferable. He attempted to produce what is in effect an international phonetic alphabet which would firstly simplify the teaching of reading, secondly enable what he calls rude, country Englishmen, as well as foreigners, to speak what is now known as Received Pronunciation, and thirdly facilitate the learning of foreign languages.

Because Hart published anonymously, his name was not known to writers of the next two centuries, and his book was not given the credit it deserves by those who benefited from its discerning analysis of

English sounds. More reference was made, in the seventeenth and eighteenth centuries, to the writings of a man less worthy of attention, William Bullokar, a schoolmaster who devoted much time and a not inconsiderable part of his limited income to the furthering of the reform cause, publishing many pamphlets and a series of translations recorded in his revised spelling. His reform is most fully elaborated in *The Booke at Large for the Amendment of Orthographie for English Speech* (1581). In the first chapter, Bullokar admitted that proposals for reform met with apathy at best and often with strenuous opposition in those who were already literate, but he proceeded nevertheless because he knew from his experience as a teacher that the traditional alphabet was unsatisfactory: 'Heereby grewe quarels in the teacher, and loth-somnesse in the learner'. His system and his arguments, however, show no advance on the work of Smith and Hart, and he remains memorable only as the first of the very many reformers remarkable for tenacity and prolificity. Contemporary with Bullokar is Richard Mulcaster, of whose book on spelling much has already been said in earlier chapters.[1] Particularly important in *The First Part of the Elementarie* is the expression of the view that traditional spelling provides English with a satisfactory writing system and is not in need of reform.[2] Rather than logical argument, Mulcaster relies in part on dogmatic conservatism,[3] but fundamentally he is arguing for consistency in the spelling of individual words as the best remedy for any faults the system may have, rather than general reform in which the inconvenience to those already literate would outweigh any gain.

After something of a hiatus, interest in reform reappeared in two of the first attempts at a description of English grammar published early

[1] Pp. 60–62 and 75–80.

[2] Mulcaster is not the first to write in opposition to reform but the first to argue against it at length. Typical of brief earlier references to the impossibility of reform is the comment by John Baret in his *Alvearie or Quadruple Dictionarie* [1580]: 'surely, we may still wonder and find fault with our Orthographie (or rather Cacographie in deed:) but it is impossible (in mine opinion) for any priuate man to amend it, vntill the learned Universities haue determined vpon the truth therof, and after the Prince also with the noble Councell, ratified and confirmed the same, to be publikely taught and vsed in the Realme' (Introduction to 'E').

[3] Consider his answer to those who aver that there are insufficient letters in the alphabet: 'This paucitie and pouertie of letters, hath contented and discharged the best, and brauest tungs, that either be, haue bene, shalbe, or can be, and hath deliuered by them, both in speche and pen, as great varietie, and as much difficultie in all arguments, and as well perceiued of all posteritie thorough their means, as possiblie can, either be deliuered, or be vnderstood, by the English tung, or yet be deuised by anie English wit' (p. 89).

8

in the seventeenth century: Alexander Gil's *Logonomia Anglica* (1619) and Charles Butler's *The English Grammar* (1633). Gil has been much praised by the most informed modern student of the orthoepists, Professor E. J. Dobson, whose comments are worth recording as they are representative of the thinking of a body of historical linguists today, and they thus illuminate current attitudes to spelling as much as seventeenth-century ones.

His system . . . was not a perfect phonetic representation of English, but it would have served as a more practical basis of a reformed spelling than any of those we have yet discussed. It was thoroughgoing and simple and did not depart too far from the old orthography. It may indeed be thought a great pity that it was not adopted, for a reform was at that time still practicable; and though it might have been found later that changes in the system were necessary, it would not have been difficult to make them. Gil's failure involved the failure of the whole movement for reform in his time.[1]

Gil is also interesting for the blame he attached to the early printers for initiating orthographic confusion in English, because they abandoned such useful graphemes as ⟨ð⟩ and ⟨ȝ⟩ and hence disrupted the one-to-one correspondence of sound and symbol. A phonemic system was his aim, but he was willing to allow departures from this to show, for example, a word's etymology or to distinguish between homophones. In the second edition of his book (published in 1621), he recommended the resurrection of ⟨ð⟩ and ⟨ȝ⟩ (for /ð/ and /dʒ/), but apart from these, together with ⟨h⟩ with a stroke through the ascender for /x/ and diaresis to show vowel length, his scheme involved the use of no new characters.[2] It was indeed a good compromise. Butler's is the last plea for general reform of spelling to spring from the earliest phase of interest in the orthography. Like Gil's, it is a compromise scheme, distinguishing homophones, indicating etymology, and departing from traditional spelling principally in the provision of new symbols for graphemes like ⟨ch⟩, ⟨th⟩, and ⟨sh⟩ (cf. Smith, p. 94), and indicating long vowels by two letters ligatured. Both Butler and Gil published their thoughts on spelling late in life (Butler was probably over seventy by 1633), by which time the interests of the majority of people exercised by the problems posed by the now fairly stable orthography had turned either to partial improvement of the system or to aids for those who found difficulty in learning it.

[1] *English Pronunciation 1500–1700*, Oxford 1968, p. 131.
[2] The stroke through ⟨h⟩ was merely carrying into print a feature common in the handwriting of the day.

Figure 4

The Ęnglifh Primrôfe.
bëa-con bec-kęn fic-ken rec-kon quic-kęn
dar-kęn hear-ken. tä-ken li-ken tô-ken
fpô-ken. Har-dęn war-dęn par-don.Hęar-
ten fhor-ten Nor-ton Môr-ton Bur-ton
but-ton mut-ton môl-tęn Bôl-ton Cä-pon
wëa-pon chëa-pęn fhä-pęn fhar-pęn Äu-
grę mâu-grę Ti-grę. Ä-cre aü-crę (aü-
chor aü ker) fe-pul-chrę. Čęn-trę mî-trę
Thë-a-trę. ox-ęn flax-ęn.

Our Fäther which art in hëavęn. 1. Hal-
lôwed bee thŷ Nämę: 2 Thŷ kiñgdom comę:
3 Thŷ wil bee dǫnę in earth, aṣ it iṣ in hëavęn : 4 Givę us thiṣ day our daily bread :
5 And forgivę us our trefpaffeṣ aṣ wee forgivę thęm that trefpaf againſt us : 6 And
lëad us not intô temptätion, but dëliver us
from evil : For thinę iṣ the kiñgdom; the
power, and the glory, for ever. Ämen.

The Bëlïëf.
I bëliëvę in God the Fäther Älmîghty,
mäker of hëavęn and earth; And in Jęſus
Chrîſt hiṣ onely Son our Lord, Which waṣ
conëcïved by the hôly Ghôſt, born of the
virğin Märïę, fuffered under Pontius Pilate,
                    H   waṣ

Richard Hodges' transition script, 1644.

The first attempt in English to simplify the earliest stages of the process of learning to read is another book by John Hart called *A Methode or Comfortable Beginning for all Vnlearned*, published in 1570, but this taught Hart's revised orthography rather than the traditional one. True aids for learners, which were intended to ease beginners into traditional spelling by teaching a compromise between this and phonemic spelling, began with the enlargement of the scope of the spelling book at the end of the sixteenth century. Edmond Coote in *The English Schoole-maister*, though he eschewed spelling reform as a general aim, asked his reader to:

marvaile not why [in the first part of the book] I haue differed in writing many syllables from the vsual manner, yea from my selfe in the rest of the worke: as *templ* without (*e*), *tun* with one (*n*) and *plums*, not *plummes* etc.; my reason is, I haue there put no moe letters then are of absolute necessitie, when in the rest I haue followed custome' (Preface).

The beginner is led from spelling which has a rough one-to-one equation with sounds into traditional orthography once he has mastered the principles of reading. Many seventeenth-century writers followed much the same practice, some being led into the suggestion that the simplified spelling might profitably be extended into general use. By far the best transition-script of the period is that proposed by Richard Hodges, again a schoolmaster, in *The English Primrose* in 1644. Hodges' compromise involves the marking of vowels with diacritics to show their quality and quantity and the underlining of graphemes which are not matched in the spoken language (see figure 4).

In the second half of the seventeenth century interest grew in the provision of an international alphabet. The idea was not new—it was implicit in Hart's work a century earlier—but it received its fullest exposition at that time, for example in William Holder's *Elements of Speech* in 1669: 'It were much to be wished, that, as there is but one single way . . . of the natural production of Letters . . . so there were throughout the world but one sort of Character for each Letter' (p. 13).[1] Two influential books of the period are John Wallis' *Grammatica Linguæ Anglicanæ* (1653) and John Wilkins' *Essay towards a Real Character and a Philosophical Language* (1668). Both men were founder-members of the Royal Society, and their works are typical of the scientific approach of the age. Wallis, a famous mathematician who

[1] By 'letters' he means sounds. It was commonly thought in the seventeenth century that sounds were identical in all languages.

was also proficient in many other fields, produced the *Grammatica* for foreigners wishing to understand English. His is the first grammar of English to try to avoid dependence on Latin grammatical analysis. The description of English sounds which forms a considerable part of the work aimed at universality in that sounds used in other languages but not heard in English are brought into his system. Wilkins, sometime Master of Trinity College, Cambridge, and later Bishop of Chester, took Wallis' 'universal' sound system a stage further by providing an international alphabet with which to represent it.[1] He was firmly of the opinion that English spelling was in need of reform, and alongside his phonetic alphabet he proposed a revised orthography for English (illustrated in figure 5) in which Greek characters supplement the roman alphabet for vowels, and the consonant symbols are extended by the liberal use of digraphs. It is a compromise between traditional and phonemic spelling, in which, for example, traditional double consonants are retained. But the zest had gone out of the reform movement, and Wilkins' revised spelling remained of academic interest. As Dr Johnson remarked nearly a century later, 'Bishop Wilkins . . . proposed, without expecting to be followed, a regular orthography'.[2]

In the eighteenth century spelling reform got a very bad press. Johnson's dismissal of Wilkins is characteristic of the attitude of the majority of his contemporaries to the preceding century's reformers. Consequently the very mild (and none too novel) modifications which Thomas Dyche would have liked to include in his spelling book published in 1723[3] (e.g. omitting ⟨e⟩ from *doctrine* or the second ⟨u⟩ from *humour*) had to be abandoned, for, as he stated in the preface, 'to propose my single Opinion against the public Vogue, I must confess, is a hazardous Enterprize; for Custom will bear a Man down, unless he find a good Number of Candid Friends to support him'. There were others of the period with slightly more temerity, 'ingenious men', as Johnson called them, who 'endeavoured to deserve well of their country, by writing *honor* and *labor* for *honour* and *labour*, *red* for *read*, in the preter-tense, *sais* for *says*, *repete* for *repeat*, *explane* for *explain*, or *declame* for *declaim*. Of these it may be said, that as they have done

---

[1] Wilkins also records his debt to Francis Lodwick, whose *An Essay towards an Universal Alphabet* was not published until the 1680s.

[2] 'A grammar of the English language', prefixed to *A Dictionary of the English Language*, 1755.

[3] *A Dictionary of all the Words Commonly Us'd in the English Tongue.*

Yur fadher huitsh art in héven, halloëd bi dhyi nàm, dhyi cingdym cym, dhyi uill bi dyn, in erth az it iz in héven, giv ys dhis dai yur daili bred, and fœrgiv ys yur trespasséz az ui fœrgiv dhem dhat trespaf against ys, and lèd ys nat intu temptasiœn, byt deliver ys frœm ivil, fœr dhyn iz dhe cingdym, dhe pyuer and dhe glœri, fœr ever and ever, Amen.

I biliv in Gœd dhe fadher almyti mäker œf héven and erth, and in Dzhezys Cryst hiz onli syn yur Lœrd, huu uaz cœnseved byi dhe holi Gost, bœrn œf dhe Virgin Màri, syffered ynder Pœnfiys Pyilat, uaz cruifiïd ded and byriëd. Hi deffended intu hel, dhe thyrd dai hi rôf again frœm dhe ded. Hi assended intu héven, huèr hi sitteth at dhe ryt hand œf Gœd dhe fadher, frœm huènf hi fhal cym tu dzhydzh dhe cuic and dhe ded. Yi biliv in dhe holi Gost, dhe holi catholic tshyrth, dhe communiœ œf Saints, dhe fœrgivnes œf sinz, de resyrrecfion œf dhe bady, and lyif everlafting. Amen.

Figure 5

John Wilkins' *Essay towards a Real Character and a Philosophical Language* (1668), lower half of page 373 from a copy now in Manchester University Library. The Lord's Prayer and the Creed are printed in Wilkins' revised spelling for English. The alternative Lord's Prayer transcription was added by an eighteenth-century owner of the book, cf. below footnote 2.

no good, they have done little harm; both because they have innovated little, and because few have followed them.'[1] Custom did indeed bear men down, with the result that less serious discussion of the reform question is recorded in the literature of eighteenth-century England than in that of any other century from the sixteenth to the twentieth.[2]

However though the debates of earlier centuries were not forgotten in the Augustan age, for the majority no advantage could be seen in reform, either wholesale or partial. To quote Johnson again:

There is in constancy and stability a general and lasting advantage, which will always overbalance the slow improvements of gradual correction. Much less ought our written language to comply with the corruptions of oral utterance, or copy that which every variation of time or place makes different from itself, and imitate those changes, which will again be changed, while imitation is employed in observing them.[3]

The growth of awareness of phonological change which resulted from diachronic linguistic studies such as that of Wallis led to insistent demands for a 'fixing' of the language, especially by means of a linguistic academy (cf. p. 81), so that writers need not fear that they

[1] *Loc. cit.*

[2] Not all men were against reform in the eighteenth century, but very few published arguments in favour of it or new revisions. That such schemes were devised in private may be seen from the eighteenth-century annotation of the copy of Wilkins' *Essay* reproduced opposite. Between the printed versions of the Lord's Prayer and the Creed in Wilkins' revised spelling an alternative Lord's Prayer transcription was added in ink by an eighteenth-century owner of the book who signed himself 'S.S.' on 4 November 1749 on the flyleaf. The alternative spellings recorded (of *which, heaven,* etc.) suggest a scheme in the process of being worked out. Like Wilkins', it is a compromise with traditional spelling (cf. the double consonants in *hallôêd* and *tréspasseʒ*). In annotations elsewhere in the book S.S. shows himself familiar with many of the early orthoepists.

[3] Preface to the dictionary. Johnson's more concise and sonorous comment in the grammar is better known: 'to accommodate orthography better to the pronunciation . . . is to measure by a shadow, to take that for a model or standard which is changing while they apply it'.

were writing in sand.[1] The linguistic area in which 'fixing' was most feasible was spelling (as the academicians in France found), and eighteenth-century Englishmen firmly rejected any attempt to undermine the one stable feature of their language. Not that the orthography was perfect, but, as James Beattie expressed it, 'Let the language . . . be fixed, as much as possible, in the phraseology, spelling, and alphabet; even though in all three respects it might have been better than it is'.[2] As Johnson's reference to 'variation of place' showed, regional and social dialect differences also posed an obstacle for reform. Jonathan Swift more than once attacked the affectations of particular groups of speakers, especially those of the modish men about town, and in *A Proposal for Correcting, Improving, and Ascertaining the English Tongue* (1712) he dwelt on the folly of reflecting such phonological variety in a phonetic spelling:

Not only the several Towns and Counties of England, have a different Way of pronouncing; but even here in *London* they clip their Words after one Manner about the Court, another in the City, and a third in the Suburbs; and in a few Years, it is probable, will all differ from themselves, as Fancy or Fashion shall direct: All which reduced to Writing, would entirely confound Orthography.

It is interesting to note that whereas earlier reformers had advocated spelling reform in order that all men might be taught to speak Received Pronunciation (cf. Hart, p. 94), the fact that they do not is here used as an argument against reform.

Apart from a general unwillingness to measure spelling by phonology, writers of the period exhibited alarm at the loss of etymological information involved in a revised spelling. Swift remarked on 'the obvious Inconvenience of utterly destroying our Etymology', and Beattie feared that reform would 'obliterate etymology'. Furthermore a growth of ambiguity was anticipated, especially in the reduction of homophones to homonyms. It was precisely such arguments in support of traditional orthography that the most distinguished advocate of

---

[1] Cf. Edmund Waller, 'Of English Verse' (*Poems*, 1668):
Poets that lasting Marble seek
Must carve in *Latine* or in *Greek*,
We write in Sand, our Language grows,
And like the Tide our work o'erflows.
Not only poets feared that their works would be incomprehensible to later ages; the replacement of Latin by English as the language of learning in the seventeenth century made it imperative that linguistic stability should be achieved. Hence the interest of the Royal Society in the question of a linguistic academy (cf. p. 81).
[2] *The Theory of Language*, 1788, p. 44.

reform in the eighteenth century set himself to answer. The man was Benjamin Franklin, philosopher, scientist and American statesman. Etymology, he suggested, is preserved in earlier literature for those who seek it, and in any case the etymology of a word is no sure guide to its current meaning. On homonymic clash, he averred that context is the guide in speech, and it is an even safer one in writing where recapitulation is easy. Franklin's interest in reform manifested itself quite late in his busy and varied life, when on 20 July 1768 he sent to a young friend in London, Mary Stevenson, his projected reformed alphabet and some material transcribed in it. The covering letter, which stated briefly the necessity for reform ('if we go on as we have done a few Centuries longer, our words will gradually cease to express Sounds, they will only stand for things, as the written words do in the Chinese Language'), is also in the new spelling. Miss Stevenson replied in the same medium, stating her objections to reform, and Franklin then wrote the now famous defence which rehearsed the lasting advantages of a reformed system.[1] The most signal of these is the increase in the proportion of the population which would be able to spell correctly.

To either you or me, who spell well in the present mode, I imagine the difficulty of changing that mode for the new is not so great, but that we might perfectly get over it in a week's writing. As to those who do not spell well, if the two difficulties are compared, (viz.) that of teaching them true spelling in the present mode, and that of teaching them the new alphabet and the new spelling according to it; I am confident that the latter would be by far the least. They naturally fall into the new method already, as much as the imperfection of their alphabet will admit of; Their present bad spelling is only bad, because contrary to the present bad rules; under the new rules it would be good. The difficulty of learning to spell well in the old way is so great, that few attain it; thousands and thousands writing on to old age, without ever being able to acquire it.

The concern that everyone should gain a facility in spelling with the minimum effort put Franklin ahead of his time. It accorded so well with the mood and aims of reformers of the second half of the nineteenth century that it was no wonder that the letter was reproduced in full in Isaac Pitman's Spelling Reform Tract no. 311 in the later 1870s (cf. p. 106). Franklin's proposal had been for a phonemically based

---

[1] The second letter was written on 28 September 1768. This, and the Stevenson letter which occasioned it, were published by Benjamin Vaughan in *Political, Miscellaneous, and Philosophical Pieces . . . by Benj. Franklin*, London 1779 (p. 472), and thus the proposals became public. The published versions of the letter have slight modification towards formality, e.g. *Dear Polly* became *Dear Madam*.

alphabet of twenty-six symbols, the traditional roman letters without ⟨c j q w x y⟩, plus six modified existing letters for sounds imperfectly represented in traditional spelling. It is possible that his experiments were influenced by Wilkins,[1] but his alphabet is quite different. Rather than Wilkins' consonant digraphs, Franklin proposed a single symbol to represent each sound, e.g. /θ/ is matched by a ligature of ⟨t⟩ and ⟨h⟩, /ð/ by one of ⟨d⟩ and ⟨h⟩, /ŋ/ by ⟨n⟩ with the tail of ⟨g⟩, and /ʃ/ by ⟨s⟩ with a vertical bar in the lower bow. He was able to confine himself to twenty-six symbols by making all the vowel graphemes serve twice, for short vowels when single and for long ones when doubled, but this led him into some phonetically undesirable pairings, e.g. an inverted ⟨h⟩, which stands for /ə/, when doubled represents /ʌ/. His far from perfect ear is shown in consonant representation too, for example in the evidence that he heard /tʃ/ and /dʒ/ as /t+ʃ/ and /d+ʃ/. Nevertheless Franklin is important in demonstrating that not all men toed the Johnsonian line in the eighteenth century, and indeed he anticipated many of the proposals and arguments put forward in the following century.

Despite the fact that Franklin intended his reformed alphabet, together with its defence, to be published, essentially it was a private scheme, worked out for the satisfaction of its author but not promulgated with the obsessiveness necessary for the successful promotion of reform. Towards the end of the eighteenth century a new series of reform proposals were published, none of which excited a great deal of public interest or acclaim, but their appearance marks the end of the hiatus in the public activity of reformers. The first of the new wave was a Scottish schoolmaster resident in London, James Elphinston, who worked for reform in a manner quite unlike that of Franklin but rather reminiscent of that of Bullokar in the energy put into the publication of his system. Between 1787 and 1795 he offered the world a series of works on grammar and spelling in a reformed script which aimed at representing the spoken language accurately (because 'orthoggraphy iz dhe *just Picture* ov Speech') but which confined itself to the characters of the roman alphabet. The system is explained in *Inglish Orthoggraphy Epittomized* (1790), from the opening page of which the above quotation is taken. Other writers were less committed, for example in America

---

[1] The suggestion is made by William B. Willcox, *The Papers of Benjamin Franklin*, vol. 15, New Haven and London 1972; the same book contains transcripts of all the relevant correspondence (pp. 173–8, 215–20) and a facsimile of the original letter.

William Thornton advocated phonemic spelling and supplied new characters for phonemes improperly represented in traditional orthography as a byproduct of his work on the teaching of the deaf.[1] William Pelham, a Boston (Massachusetts) bookseller, proposed in *A System of Notation* (1808) the indication of pronunciation in writing by the use of a complicated system of diacritics.[2] While none of these schemes is intrinsically very interesting, their publication suggests that the basic assumptions of the eighteenth century were being questioned. Gradually the pendulum swung, the majority of writers on the subject of spelling coming to favour revision of the system rather than the stability preferred by Johnson and his contemporaries. Noah Webster's early writings, considered in detail on page 83, are symptomatic of the change which took place in the attitude of linguists and educationalists: in 1783 he was a determined anti-reformer,[3] but in 1789 he began the long career as a reform campaigner which was to make his name one of the best remembered of all those associated with the history of spelling.

The changed mood by which reform was looked on with favour at the end of the eighteenth century was the result of a revolution in educational philosophy based on the writings of Jean-Jacques Rousseau. The rigid learning-by-rote approach of the eighteenth-century grammarians was overthrown in favour of an appeal to children's natural curiosity and intelligence. The ability to read, central to all education, could not be acquired—indeed, could be hindered—by the application of commonsense to the traditional spelling system with its inadequacy in phonemic representation, and consequently the idea of an orthographic revision which made the representation more systematic and hence more logical gained increasing support. Other factors influenced the growth of interest in reform in the early nineteenth century. For example, missionary contact with non-literate societies led to the evolution of alphabets, inevitably phonemic, by

[1] *Cadmus, A Treatise on the Elements of Written Language*, Philadelphia, 1793.

[2] Enos Weed published *The American Orthography, in three books* in 1797–8, the third book consisting of a reformed orthography, but no surviving copy has been traced. Cf. R. C. Alston, *A Bibliography of the English Language*, vol. 4 Spelling Books (Bradford 1967), item 941.

[3] Cf.: 'Our language is indeed pronounced very differently from the spelling; this is an inconvenience we regret, but cannot remedy. To attempt progressive change, is idle; it will keep the language in perpetual fluctuation without an effectual amendment. And to attempt a total change at once, is equally idle and extravagant, as it would render the language unintelligible' (*Grammatical Institute*, p. 11 footnote).

WYTHEVILLE COMMUNITY
COLLEGE LIBRARY
WYTHEVILLE, VIRGINIA

means of which the Bible might be made available to converts, and
attempts to pattern the new orthographies on existing ones emphasised
that the roman alphabet as used in English had a confused relationship
with the English sound-system. Similarly, growth in the popularity
of shorthand systems with a phonetic base highlighted the anomalies
of traditional spelling. But the main impulse for reformation throughout
the nineteenth and twentieth centuries has remained the need felt
by educationalists for a simplification of the difficulties observed in
learning to read.

The main British champion of reform throughout the major part of
the nineteenth century was Isaac Pitman, who in 1837 at the age of
24 created the shorthand which bears his name. Shorthand systems
were common enough in the two preceding centuries, but the new
element in Pitman's was that it was based on phonetic principles,[1] and
it was from this concern with the representation of sounds on paper
that Pitman moved into reform of traditional spelling. In 1842 the
first volume of his *Phonographic Journal* (one of many periodicals which
he published during a prolific writing career)[2] offered a phonemic
alphabet of new characters, but this was soon seen to be too extreme
and in *The Phonotypic Journal* in the following two years an extended
roman alphabet called Phonotype was proposed and gradually
amended by Pitman and his principal collaborator of the time, A. J.
Ellis. What evolved by 1870 was the alphabet of thirty-eight characters
which appears in figure 6.[3] For much of the nineteenth century, the
publishing organisation which was built around the alphabet, The
Reading, Writing, and Spelling Reform, issued from its impressive
building in Bath a continuous stream of books in the new spelling
(including the Bible) and of pamphlets advocating it. Financial support came from the commercially successful shorthand publications
(which the Reform, incidentally, helped to publicise) and from public

[1] A phonetic shorthand was invented by Wilkins in 1668 but like his other alphabets
it gained no general currency (cf. p. 99).

[2] *The Phonographic Journal* appeared for three years and then merged into *The
Phonographic Correspondent* which survived until 1858. Then *The Phonographic Magazine*
appeared for five years. Meanwhile *The Phonotypic Journal*, which was first issued in
1843 under the same cover as *The Phonographic Journal*, appeared continuously under
various names (e.g. *The Phonetic Journal*, *Pitman's Journal*) until well into the twentieth
century.

[3] Phonotype was established in 1847 (on the earlier history of the Pitman-Ellis
collaboration, see *The Phonetic Journal* for January, 1848). Between 1847 and 1870 no
less than eighty-eight new characters were experimented with.

Figure 6

4
THE PHONETIC ALPHABET.

The phonetic letters in the first column are pronounced like the italic letters in the words that follow. The last column contains the names *of the letters.*

CONSONANTS.				Liquids.		
Mutes.			L l	fa*ll*		el
P p	ro*pe*	pi	R r	*r*a*r*e		ar
B b	ro*b*e	bi	*Coalescents.*			
T t	fa*t*e	ti	W w	*w*et		wɛ
D d	fa*d*e	di	Y y	*y*et		yɛ
C ᵷ	e*tch*	ᵷɛ	*Aspirate.*			
J j	e*dge*	jɛ	H h	*h*ay		ɛᵷ
K k	lee*k*	kɛ	VOWELS.			
G g	lea*gue*	gɛ	*Guttural.*			
Continuants.			A a	*a*m		at
F f	sa*fe*	ef	ꓮ ꞻ	*a*lms		ꞻ
V v	sa*v*e	vi	E e	*e*ll		et
ꓤ ꜰ	wrea*th*	iꜰ	Ɛ ɛ	*a*le		ɛ
ꓸ ꝺ	wrea*the*	ꝺi	·I i	*i*ll		it
S s	hi*ss*	es	Ꞁ i	*ee*l		i
Z z	hi*s*	zi	*Labial.*			
Σ ʃ	vi*ci*ous	iʃ	O o	*o*n		ot
Ꙅ ʒ	vi*si*on	ʒi	ꙩ ꙩ	*a*ll		ꙩ
Nasals.			Ꙭ Ꙭ	*u*p		Ꙭt
M m	see*m*	em	Ꙩ σ	*o*pe		σ
N n	see*n*	en	U u	f*u*ll		ut
ꙍ ŋ	si*ng*	iŋ	ꙍ ꙍ	f*oo*d		ꙍ

DIPHTHONGS: Ɨ ɨ, Ꙋ ꙋ, OU ou, OI oi.
as heard in by, new, now, boy.

A ¼lb. parcel of Tracts explanatory of Phonetic Shorthand and Phonetic Printing, may be had from I. Pitman, Phonetic Institute, Bath; post-paid, 6d.

Isaac Pitman's Phonotype as developed by 1870.

subscription which ranged from very generous sums from individuals to modest contributions from large numbers of the general public. The involvement of so many laymen in the project shows the success Pitman had in raising spelling reform to the status of a popular issue, but it was also a serious academic one, involving philologists of the stature of Max Müller, who pledged his support for Pitman's scheme in *The Fortnightly Review* for April, 1876. Pitman frequently reiterated that his concern was for the simplification of reading, to be effected by making spelling phonemic, that 'the education of the poor' might be 'rendered not only possible, but easy' (advertisement for publications of the Reform). He was rewarded by the backing of the teaching profession: in 1876 the National Union of Elementary Teachers passed a resolution calling for a Royal Commission to consider the question of spelling reform.

Meanwhile similar pressures were building up in America, where again the principal concern was over the waste of energy and expense involved in the teaching of spelling. Pitman's reference to the education of the poor is to be associated with Britain's 1870 Education Act which provided education for all; in the United States the authorities were concerned to provide education for a heterogeneous population, one sixth of whom were first or second generation immigrants, mostly non-English speaking, and the teaching of English both spoken and written became associated with the welding of a single nation. The question of reform exercised all concerned with education from members of the Bureau of Education right down to practising schoolteachers. One of the most successful experiments with a teaching alphabet was initiated by Edwin Leigh of St Louis in 1866. This employed hairline type for 'silent' letters and modified forms for others, thus allowing for transference to traditional spelling after the initial stages of learning to read were passed. It was used in a large number of schools in the St Louis area for more than twenty years.[1] Figure 7 reproduces an example so that its analogies with other experiments of a similar kind may be seen.[2] More important in its longterm consequences was the movement for reform associated with the universities, where Francis

---

[1] Cf. *The Spelling Reform*, Bureau of Education Circular of Information no. 8, 1893, pp. 7 ff.

[2] That such a scheme was seriously considered in England also may be seen in the fact that the Rev. J. Rice Byrne, Inspector of Schools in Great Britain, proposed to the Education Committee in 1868 that a teaching alphabet be compulsorily introduced into all state elementary schools.

Figure 7

100 Eclectic Primary Reader.

and jump and frisk about′ as though he were very happy, as no doubt he is.

6. One day Dash came trotting up stairs with a fine large pear in his mouth.

7. He held it by the stem, and looked up at James, as much as to say, "Dear master, I have got something very nice for you."

8. James rose up in the bed, and reached out his hand for the pear. Dash gave it to him, and as James said, "Thank you, Dash," the dog barked, as much as to say, "You are very welcome," and bounded out of the room.

9. Is not Dash a fine dog? I am sure James will be kinder to him than ever when he gets well.

Edwin Leigh's transition script, 1866. Note the subtleties such as two varieties of ⟨s⟩ for /s/ and /z/, and two of ⟨e⟩ for /e/ and /iː/.

March, a prominent philologist, with colleagues such as S. S. Haldeman and W. D. Whitney, founded the American Spelling Reform Association in 1876 as an offshoot of the American Philological Association. Their aim was to break down the barrier of prejudice which had so far prevented any reform scheme from being generally adopted, and to produce a modified roman alphabet which would represent English phonemically. The alphabet (of thirty-two letters) did appear, together with suggestions for a transition programme from the traditional to the new, but little progress was made with its promulgation.

Things were moving at much the same pace in England, where the British Philological Society, headed by A. H. Sayce, Henry Sweet and James Murray, had already shown interest in the matter. As early as 1869 the Society's Council decided that reform was desirable, and appointed a committee 'to consider [its] direction, extent, and nature'. Its members were unable to agree. One of them, Pitman's collaborator Ellis, produced on his own account a revised spelling with minimum disturbance which he called Glossic: 'a new system of spelling, intended to be used concurrently with the existing English orthography in order to remedy some of its defects, without changing its form, or detracting from its value'.[1] It arose out of Ellis' work on the history of pronunciation, and it was hoped that the script might be useful in teaching children to read. Objections to it as too extreme led to the production in 1880 of a transition stage between it and traditional spelling called Dimidiun, but this aroused even less enthusiasm than Glossic. The importance of Glossic, however, is that it marked a change in direction of the movement; from the date of its introduction (1871) most reformers concentrated on a minimum disturbance reform confined to the letters of the roman alphabet. The British Spelling Reform Association was founded in 1879 and included not only eminent linguists but celebrities like Tennyson and Darwin. The British Association, not content with the many orthographies already in existence (including those invented by its own members like Sweet, Ellis and D. P. Fry) proposed new reform schemes (three within six years), and the whole movement would have fragmented had not an element of cohesion been achieved when Sweet and the Americans

---

[1] The quotation, and details of Glossic, may be found prefixed to volume III of *Early English Pronunciation*, published by the Early English Text Society in 1871 (Extra Series 14). For the five volumes of *Early English Pronunciation* itself, Ellis invented another alphabet, Palaeotype, which used roman alphabet letters but in a variety of type faces to represent different sounds.

collaborated in a scheme for the amendment of the worst anomalies in the traditional system. This recommended, in a series of twenty-four rules, such changes as the dropping of 'superfluous' letters (*liv, fether, gess, actin, tripl*) and minor adaptations which would not confuse readers familiar with traditional forms (*abuv, fonetic, flasht*). The scheme found favour with academics on both sides of the Atlantic and for more than twenty years such forms were occasionally used in their printed material (they were especially common in books by philologists addressed to philologists), but, despite official backing of the reform by the U.S. Federal Government, the general public could not be persuaded of its value.

In the twentieth century new impetus was given to the reform movement by the setting up in the United States of the Simplified Spelling Board in 1906 with the help of a quarter of a million dollars from the philantropist Andrew Carnegie. The Board's aim was basically to continue the work of the Reform Association and promote the simplified spelling of relatively common words recommended by March and Sweet. The American movement has since been fairly passive, despite the appearance alongside the Board of sister organisations: the Simplified Spelling League and the Simpler Spelling Association. Almost contemporary with the founding of the Board was the formation of the British Simplified Spelling Society, a body which has remained rather more active, with important revivals in the twenties and forties. Notwithstanding its long life, however, the multiplicity of approaches which has always been one of the principal bugbears of reformers has resulted in no one set of proposals being maintained for very long, and the concord with the Americans which has often been aimed at has rarely been fully realised. The Society from its foundation enjoyed the support of academics, for example Walter Skeat, F. J. Furnivall and James Murray in its early days, Gilbert Murray and Walter Ripman later, but it has been successful too in involving public figures such as Baden-Powell and industrialists like Sir George Hunter of Messrs Swan Hunter. As with the earlier Reform Associations and with the contemporary American movements, the aim was the promulgation of a revision based on the existing alphabet. The scheme adopted at first was Simplified Spelling, which was used in the publication of much of the Society's material, for example in its periodical *Pioneer ov Simplified Spelling* (1912–18). By 1926 when the *Pioneer* was revived for two years (as *The Pioneer of Reformed Spelling*,

9

printed largely in traditional orthography), strict adherence to Simplified Spelling had been dropped in favour of any reform which seemed likely to improve the sound-symbol relationship of English without departing from the existing alphabet. Consequently considerable support was given by the Society, and also by the American Board, to R. E. Zachrisson's Anglic, a reform with minimum disturbance which aimed at generalising the most common of existing graphemes for each phoneme, and which, in its author's words, 'practicaly agrees with the prezent orthografy in mor than haaf the numbr ov the words ocurring on wun printid padge'.[1] Out of Anglic and its modifications grew the Simplified Spelling Society's new scheme in 1941, New Spelling (Nue Speling). This and Dr Axel Wijk's Regularized Inglish (1959), which is also a system involving minimum disturbance and is based on a statistical survey of traditional spelling, are explained in detail in the first volume of the Mont Follick series, *Alphabets for English*.[2] The main difference between them has been stated concisely by Wijk: 'the principles of Regularized Inglish enable us to retain the present spelling in over 90 per cent of the vocabulary, whereas the *New Spelling* of the Simplified Spelling Society only preserves it in about 10 per cent or less of the words'.[3] The truth of the claim may be tested by comparison of a few sentences transcribed in each.

Nue Speling:

At dhe furst glaans a pasej in eny reformd speling looks 'kweer' or 'ugly'. Dhis objekshon iz aulwaez dhe furst to be maed; it iz purfektly natueral; it iz dhe hardest to remuuv. Indeed, its efekt iz not weekend until dhe nue speling iz noe longger nue, until it haz been seen ofen enuf to be familyar.

Regularized Inglish:

At the first glaance a passage in eny reformd spelling looks 'queer' and 'ugly'. This objection iz aulwayz the first to be made; it iz perfectly natural; it iz the hardest to remoove. Indeed, its effect iz not weekend until the new spelling iz no longer new, until it haz been seen offen enuff to be familiar.

On the revisions of Nue Speling was based the latest in the long line of transition scripts intended to help children overcome the initial difficulties of learning to read: Sir James Pitman's initial teaching

---

[1] 'Anglic and the Anglic Muuvment', *Simplified English Spelling* published by the Simplified Spelling Society, 1930, p. 11.
[2] Ed. W. Haas, Manchester 1969.
[3] *Op. cit.*, p. 61.

alphabet (i.t.a.). Unlike Nue Speling however, i.t.a. is not confined to the roman alphabet, as its original name, the Augmented Roman Alphabet, indicates. In it a number of ligatures and adapted roman characters are introduced to provide a phonemic alphabet with a potential for easy transference to traditional orthography. They are illustrated in the following sample, the first to reach a wide public in 1960.[1]

ſhis is printed in an augmented rœman alfabet, ſhe purpos ov whiȼh is not, as miet bee suppœsd, tω reform our spelliŋ, but tω imprωv ſhe lerniŋ ov reediŋ. it is intended ſhat when ſhe beginner has aȼheevd ſhe iniſhial sucsess ov flωensy in ſhis speſhially eesy form, his fuetuer progress ſhωd bee confiend tω reediŋ in ſhe present alfabets and spelliŋs ov ſhem œnly.

Like many of the similar experiments which preceded it, i.t.a. was at first very popular and successful, especially after it was given the blessing of the Ministry of Education, but the seemingly inevitable public rejection of what is 'queer or ugly', coupled with growing informed objections to it,[2] seem likely to send it the way of its forebears.

To complete the picture of twentieth-century reform, reference must be made to two men who attempted to further the reform cause by large bequests. Bernard Shaw campaigned long and hard for an entirely new alphabet not necessarily to oust the roman one but to be used alongside it by professional writers who, by virtue of the unnecessary effort entailed in communicating by traditional spelling, were, to use his own term, 'manual labourers'. His will provided for the creation and promotion of a newly designed set of forty characters to be used in strict one-to-one correspondence with speech sounds, and in 1962 Penguin Books published a version of *Androcles and the Lion* with parallel texts in the Shaw and roman alphabets. A quarterly news-sheet *Shaw-script* was subsequently begun by one of the designers of the script, Kingsley Read.[3] The other spelling benefactor of our age is Mont Follick, who also spent much of his public life advocating reform, this time within the confines of the roman alphabet. His own revision was intended primarily to help literate foreigners to learn English, as like Zachrisson, the creator of Anglic, he was concerned

[1] I. J. Pitman, 'Learning to Read: an Experiment', *Journal of the Royal Society of Arts* February 1961 and later printed separately.

[2] Cf. W. Haas, *Phono-graphic Translation*, Manchester 1970, especially pp. 53–6 and references.

[3] The Shaw alphabet and its creation are described in P. A. D. MacCarthy, 'The Bernard Shaw Alphabet', *Alphabets for English*, pp. 105–17.

9*

with the role of English as a world language,[1] but his system suffered from the fact that it was not published until twenty years after it was composed in 1914, by which time rather better revisions along the same lines (e.g. Anglic) had appeared.[2] At the end of his life, Follick conceived the idea of founding a university chair, so that his work on spelling might be continued. Part of the result of the bequest, subsequent to his death in 1958, to the University of Manchester is this series of studies which bears his name.

The prominence of the names of so many of the most famous linguists of the late nineteenth and early twentieth centuries in the lists of members of the Reform Associations and the Simplified Spelling movements should not disguise the fact that not all academics were either convinced of the need for extensive reform of spelling or agreed on the means of achieving even marginal orthographic improvements. Some of the blame for the lack of public or official response to the call for reform must be put down to the diversity of schemes proposed, but though such diversity undoubtedly had disadvantages, it did lead to more attention being given to the principles on which reform should be based, and thus to the relationship between speech and writing. In the twentieth century it is possible to trace the development of a school of thought which is not so much anti-reformist as fearful of too radical or precipitous a reform, being disturbed by the easy assumption of men of the nineteenth century that writing should reflect speech. The foundation of this school was laid by Henry Bradley in a paper 'On the Relations between Spoken and Written Language, with special reference to English', read at the International Historical Congress in April, 1913.[3] The opening sentences reached to the heart of the matter:

Many of the advocates of spelling reform are in the habit of asserting, as if it were an axiom admitting of no dispute, that the sole function of writing is to represent sounds. It appears to me that this is one of those spurious truisms that are not intelligently believed by any one, but which continue to be repeated because nobody takes the trouble to consider what they really mean.

[1] This is a theme often rehearsed by twentieth-century reform writers, even to the present day. Cf. Wijk: 'the adoption ov such a system ov spelling az Regularized Inglish . . . wood remoove the principal obstacle that prevents Inglish from becumming a truly international language' (*Alphabets for English*, p. 61).
[2] For a summary of Follick's work and an illustration of his scheme, see Sir James Pitman, 'The late Dr. Mont Follick—an appraisal', *Alphabets for English*, pp. 14–49.
[3] The paper was printed in *Proceedings of the British Academy*, vol. VI, and reprinted separately by Clarendon Press in 1919.

Bradley's thesis is that writing's capacity for conveying meaning does not depend on its accuracy as a reflection of speech, and that such accuracy may even be a disadvantage in the case of homonymic clash. Written English contains features which are phonetically useless (e.g. capitalisation, punctuation), and much technical and scientific terminology is 'primarily graphic' in that it never forms part of the spoken language. Most important of all, the written language is partly ideographic: 'The group of letters, seen as a whole, enables us to identify the word intended, and having thus identified it we pronounce it from habit. Even if the word is quite new to us—a proper name, for instance—the syllable, rather than the letter, is the unit present to consciousness.' However, he recognised that though a partly ideographic spelling has advantages for 'the educated adult', the unphonetic features add enormously to the difficulty of learning to read and write. He admitted that partial reform of the system may be necessary, and expanded this line of thought in a later appendix in which the prime target for such reform is homographs like *read, bow* and *lead*. But a move into phonetic spelling generally he saw as leading to wider linguistic change than the reformers were aware of, in particular in the discarding of many of the homophones in the language (when they become homographs also) and in a reduction of English's dependence on classical borrowings for expansion of its lexicon.

Bradley's arguments were selectively used by such strident opponents of reform as George Saintsbury, Professor of Rhetoric and English Literature at Edinburgh University, but more important than their effect on conservative opinion is the use made of them by later linguists. One such, Sir William Craigie, like Bradley an editor of the *Oxford English Dictionary*, wrote two Society for Pure English tracts on the subject of spelling. The first, *Some Anomalies of Spelling* (no. 59, published in 1942), illustrated inconsistencies within the main types of spellings, which he defined as native, classical or French, and exotic, and suggested minor changes which would iron out the anomalies without any great disturbance of the orthography as a whole. His awareness of Bradley's view is shown at the end of his paper where he throws doubt on the 'commonly assumed . . . self-evident axiom that a phonetic spelling, or some near approach to this, must necessarily be the most suitable for any language, without regard to its character or history' (p. 332). It is this doubt which is enlarged upon in his second tract, *Problems of Spelling Reform* (no. 63, 1944). Among the problems he lists society's opposition or indifference to the schemes of four centuries, and the commercial considerations of those engaged in the production of printed matter. But the real crux as he saw it is that 'no language can free itself from its history' (p. 50). Spelling reform must take account of the ideographic nature of written English for a literate reader, and reformers should be aware of distinctions between written and spoken morphology (e.g. a single written plural marker ⟨s⟩ may have advantages over the spoken morpheme which varies phonetically according to context: /s, z, ɪz/). Successful reform would remove the international character of many written words, especially those with cognates in the Romance languages, and would make homophones homographs also, necessitating the revision of all existing dictionaries not just from the point of view of spelling but in the organisation of the lemmata (an important commercial consideration).

Others in our own day have followed what is in essence the Bradley approach. Professor J. Vachek has for some years been advocating the examination of the value of traditional orthography in a larger linguistic context than that of its relationship with the phonological system,[1] and more recently Professor Haas has emphasised that 'various non-phonological factors need to be taken account of . . . We shall often find it advantageous for an orthography to deviate from a phonetically faithful representation of speech.'[2] Thus in contrast to the unanimous resolution of the Philological Society in 1868 in favour of some form of reform, today just a century later many linguists find themselves working towards precisely the opposite conclusion, that traditional orthography is the optimal writing system for English. The nearest approach to such a standpoint is made by prominent members of the generative/transformational school. Noam Chomsky and Morris Halle maintain in *The Sound Pattern of English*[3] that it is not the function of writing to represent speech. Without acknowledging the work of earlier labourers in the field, they echo Bradley in suggesting that 'an optimal orthography would have one representation for each lexical entry' (except, as they say, for 'unpredictable variants' such as *man–men*, *buy–bought*), and they virtually repeat Craigie in saying that since 'orthography is a system designed for readers who know the language

[1] Cf. 'Some Remarks on Writing and Phonetic Transcription' (1949), reprinted in *Readings in Linguistics*, ed. E. P. Hamp, Chicago 1966.
[2] *Phono-graphic Translation*, pp. 3–4.
[3] New York, Evanston and London 1968. The most important passages occur on pp. 49 ff. and 184 ff.

... it would be quite pointless for [it] to indicate ... predictable variants' such as the phonetically variable plural marker. The 'noteworthy, but not too surprising' conclusion is 'that English orthography, despite its often cited inconsistencies, comes remarkably close to being an optimal orthographic system for English'. Even if reflection of speech were to be desired, 'English orthography ... turns out to be rather close to the true phonological representation, given the nonlinguistic constraints that must be met by a spelling system, namely, that it utilize a uni-dimensional linear representation and that it limit itself essentially to the letters of the Latin alphabet'. A simple example may explain this view: in *divine, serene, profane* (seen against *divinity, serenity, profanity*), the diphthongs and long vowels /aɪ/, /iː/, /eɪ/ are indicated in the orthography by ⟨e⟩ after the single consonant, a device which is possible because the sound /e/ is 'the only vowel which does not appear in final position phonetically'.

And so the debate continues. In a recent *Times Literary Supplement* editorial comment on Shaw's desire for reform, the view was expressed that 'the case for change [in spelling] should be made regularly, forcefully, and audibly' (2 June 1972, p. 633). It certainly has been for the last two centuries, if not for the last four. What is most needed at the present time, however, is not simply a repetition of the arguments of earlier generations of reformers but more information about the relative value of existing orthographies, be they traditional, phonetic, or compromise. The same TLS writer also suggested that Government might take a hand in imposing a spelling reform: 'We are no longer incapable of making radical change. We have modified our currency, and there are very great advantages to be gained from reformed spelling.' If we take this suggestion seriously, then the more information on the subject which is available, the more capable the community will be of ensuring that the right decision on the question is taken. Despite vast amounts of time and money spent on examining English spelling in the twentieth century, it is remarkable how much of what has been written is not new but is a reiteration, whether the authors know it or not, of what has been said before. Since 1568 many different orthographies for English have been experimented with, and since the Middle Ages traditional spelling itself has grown organically, and perhaps less haphazardly than is often supposed. A little more awareness of the history of English spelling and of attempts at its reform will not come amiss in contemporary discussion of the state of our orthography.

Bibliography

There is no comprehensive study of the history of English spelling. The spelling of individual words is given detailed consideration in
The Oxford English Dictionary, ed. James A. Murray, *et al.*, 12 vols plus Supplement, Oxford 1933 (Second Supplement, ed. R. W. Burchfield, Oxford 1972-),
and general comments on the history and use of each letter prefix each section of the work. A brief outline of the history of English spelling is to be found in
G. H. Vallins, *Spelling*, second ed. revised by D. G. Scragg, London 1965
and in most histories of the English language of which the following are a representative sample:
A. C. Baugh, *A History of the English Language*, second ed., London 1959
G. L. Brook, *A History of the English Language*, London 1958
Simeon Potter, *Our Language*, Penguin Books 1950
Thomas Pyles, *The Origins and Development of the English Language*, New York 1964
Barbara M. H. Strang, *A History of English*, London 1970
C. L. Wrenn, *The English Language*, London 1949.
Studies of the history of phonology illustrate the history of spelling incidentally, especially
Karl Luick, *Historische Grammatik der englischen Sprache*, Leipzig 1914-40.
The following books may be consulted for enlargement of and, in some cases, justification for statements made in the text. The list is divided into chapters for convenience, books relating to material of more than one chapter being included at the earliest appropriate place. Where the topic enlarged upon is not apparent in the title a reference is appended in square brackets. Primary sources and books and articles dealing with points of very minor detail are excluded since full reference to them is given in footnotes to the text.
Chapter 1
A. Campbell, *Old English Grammar*, Oxford 1959
Margaret Deansley, *The Pre-Conquest Church in England*, second ed., London 1963
Ralph W. V. Elliott, *Runes*, Manchester 1959
W. Keller, *Angelsächsische Palaeographie*, Berlin 1906
N. R. Ker, *Catalogue of Manuscripts containing Anglo-Saxon*, Oxford 1957
Randolph Quirk and C. L. Wrenn, *An Old English Grammar*, London 1955

Karl Brunner, *Altenglische Grammatik nach der angelsächsischen Grammatik von Eduard Sievers*, third ed., Tübingen 1965

F. M. Stenton, *Anglo-Saxon England*, Oxford 1943

Chapter 2

S. T. R. O. d'Ardenne, þe *Liflade ant te Passiun of Seinte Iuliene*, Liege 1936

Karl Brunner, *An Outline of Middle English Grammar*, translated by G. K. W. Johnson, Oxford 1963

R. W. Burchfield, 'The language and orthography of the Ormulum MS', *Transactions of the Philological Society* 1956, pp. 56–87

Cecily Clark, *The Peterborough Chronicle 1070–1154*, second ed., Oxford 1970

E. Ekwall, *Studies on the Population of Medieval London*, Lund 1956

Jacek Fisiak, *A Short Grammar of Middle English*, London 1968

F. E. Harmer, *Anglo-Saxon Writs*, Manchester 1952 [Old English chancery spelling]

Charles Jones, *An Introduction to Middle English*, New York 1972

Richard Jordan, *Handbuch der mittelenglischen Grammatik*, Heidelberg 1925

H. R. Loyn, *The Norman Conquest*, London 1965

Angus McIntosh, 'The analysis of written Middle English', *Transactions of the Philological Society* 1956, pp. 26–55

„ 'A new approach to Middle English dialectology', *English Studies* 44 (1963), pp. 1–11

Fernand Mossé, *A Handbook of Middle English*, translated by James A. Walker, Baltimore 1952

M. L. Samuels, 'Some applications of Middle English dialectology', *English Studies* 44 (1963), pp. 81–94

Chapter 3

Norman Davis, 'Scribal variation in late fifteenth-century English', *Mélanges de Linguistique et de Philologie: Fernand Mossé in Memoriam*, Paris 1959, pp. 95–103

Otto Jespersen, *A Modern English Grammar on Historical Principles*, part I Sounds and Spellings, third ed., Heidelberg 1922

John M. Manly and Edith Rickert, *The Text of the Canterbury Tales*, vol. I Descriptions of the Manuscripts, Chicago 1940 [fifteenth-century spelling]

M. K. Pope, *From Latin to Modern French with especial consideration of Anglo-Norman*, Manchester 1934

W. Rothwell, 'The teaching of French in medieval England', *The Modern Language Review* 63 (1968), pp. 37–46

J. Vising, *Anglo-Norman Language and Literature*, London and Oxford 1923

Chapter 4

E. J. Dobson, *English Pronunciation 1500–1700*, second ed., Oxford 1968

A. J. Ellis, *Early English Pronunciation*, vol. III, Early English Text Society Extra Series 14, London 1871

Richard Foster Jones, *The Triumph of the English Language*, Stanford 1953

Chapter 5

H. S. Bennett, *English Books and Readers 1475 to 1557*, Cambridge 1952

„ *English Books and Readers 1558 to 1603*, Cambridge 1965

H. S. Bennett, *English Books and Readers 1603 to 1640*, Cambridge 1970

N. F. Blake, *Caxton and his World*, London 1969

Giles E. Dawson and Laetitia Kennedy-Skipton, *Elizabethan Handwriting 1500–1650*, London 1968

W. W. Greg, 'An Elizabethan printer and his copy', *The Library* fourth series 4 (1923–4), pp. 102–118

Charlton Hinman, *The Printing and Proof-reading of the First Folio of Shakespeare*, Oxford 1963

N. E. Osselton, 'Formal and informal spelling in the eighteenth century', *English Studies* 44 (1963), pp. 267–75

A. C. Partridge, 'Shakespeare's orthography in *Venus and Adonis* and some early quartos', *Shakespeare Survey* 7 (1954), pp. 35–47

Alfred W. Pollard, 'Elizabethan spelling as a literary and bibliographical clue', *The Library* fourth series 4 (1923–4), pp. 1–8

E. Rudolf, *Die englische Orthographie von Caxton bis Shakespeare*, Marburg 1904

Percy Simpson, *Proof-reading in the Sixteenth, Seventeenth and Eighteenth Centuries*, London 1935

Chapter 6

R. C. Alston, *A Bibliography of the English Language from the Invention of Printing to the year 1800*, especially vol. 4 Spelling Books, Bradford 1967

T. R. Lounsbury, *English Spelling and Spelling Reform*, New York 1909

Susie I. Tucker, *English Examined: Two Centuries of Comment on the Mother-tongue*, Cambridge 1961 [seventeenth- and eighteenth-century attitudes]

R. E. Zachrisson, 'Four hundred years of English spelling reform', *Studia Neophilologica* 4 (1931–2), pp. 1–69.

Word index

A list of Modern English words the history of which is discussed in the text.

n = footnote.

Subject index